Helen Braid was an A... moved 23 times by t... ...w lives in Midlothian. She is marri..., with one son recently graduated and one at secondary school. She has worked as a teacher, research fellow, university lecturer, educational psychologist and freelance journalist. The common thread in all her work is finding words to record and reflect other people's experiences. She has published several non-fiction books including a language scheme for schools, as well as many academic papers and feature articles. For nine years she has been recovering from ME, but a return to full-time academic work provoked a major relapse and the final stages of this anthology were completed from her bed. Her fictionalised autobiography, *Letters to My Semi-Detached Son: A Mother's Story*, was published by The Women's Press in 1993.

Also by Helen Braid from The Women's Press:

Letters to My Semi-Detached Son: A Mother's Story (1993)

A Stranger at My Table

women write about mothering adolescents

HELEN BRAID, EDITOR

First published by The Women's Press Ltd, 1997
A member of the Namara Group
34 Great Sutton Street, London EC1V 0DX

British Library Cataloguing-in-Publication Data
A catalogue record for this book is available from the British Library

ISBN 0 7043 4472 6

Typeset in Bembo by The Harrington Consultancy
Printed and bound in Great Britain by BPC Paperbacks

For Gwen Gray

Acknowledgements

It has been such a pleasure to work on this book because communicating and working with the contributors has brought a whole new network of invisible friends. I want to thank them all for their patience while the book took shape. Behind any writer there are always others who offer invaluable support: Kathy Gale at The Women's Press who worked with me with such sensitivity and skill first on *Letters to My Semi-Detached Son*, and then on this anthology; Meg Graham who has propped me up personally and professionally throughout this project; my husband who remains a tower of strength. Finally, a big thank you and an even bigger hug for my two sons whose teenage trauma, door-banging, and honesty inspired this and the previous book.

Contents

Preface

Five years ago, when I was trying to make sense of my first son's adolescence, I thought I was the only mother who was finding the teenage years impossible. For us, finally, there came a point when our relationship was unbearable and the tension in our family was damaging every one of us. The roots of the breakdown between my son and myself trailed back many, many years, but during adolescence unresolved anger and pain turned him into a hostile stranger who perfected the art of total passive resistance. I had lost him. When he was fifteen years old I put him and his backpack on a train and sent him to live with his father two hundred miles away. Then I wrote him letters which I never sent, but which became a book published by The Women's Press (*Letters to My Semi-Detached Son*, 1993). The book prompted some controversial press, but in many, many personal letters, and afterwards, in support groups which my friend Meg Graham and I ran, I heard other mothers saying the same things. All of them asked 'Am I the only one going through this?' Many of them carried an enormous burden of guilt and blame for what their teenage children were doing. Most felt failures as mothers. And so when the support groups stopped (because Meg became pregnant with what were to be twin boys, and I started a full-time research job working with teenagers!) this book began.

Now, with my second son aged fifteen, I am reflecting on the past. I am appalled at what happened with my first-born and at the same time accept its inevitability. Parting with my younger one — no matter what he might do — is unthinkable. I am watching him cope with the awkwardness of the teenage years with feelings of respect, amusement, sympathy, admiration and love. His brief door-slamming episodes barely make an impact on the bond between us. Yes, he annoys me sometimes, but afterwards I can smile and, just as significantly, my feelings for my elder son have also changed in ways I once would have thought impossible. So this feels like a good emotional place to be for editing this book because I can look both ways. I have experienced the pain of mothering an adolescent, and I also know its pleasures. I want this anthology to blow the lid off the hidden bewilderment, isolation and powerlessness which so many women feel. But I also want to celebrate the positive experiences which many women acknowledge when they write about the satisfaction, support and love they have received from their teenage children.

At first I was worried that other women would not want to write about their experiences. It is one thing to share with a friend the trials and tribulations of your child's teenage years, it is quite another to put pen to paper and go public. But this is exactly what mothers have done. I placed an advert about the idea for the anthology in a couple of newspapers and journals, alerted my network of women writers, and the letters requesting more information (and telling me life stories) started to flood in. I sent out about 350 fliers and more than a hundred submissions came back, varying in style and presentation from biro on lined paper to glossy pieces in coloured folders to contributions from established writers. I read them all. All except one were from women (the man sent an inappropriate newspaper cutting). Pieces about sons outnumbered pieces about daughters by about six to one. A large proportion were from single parents. Taken together, what was wonderful about these contributions was the way they depicted a whole spectrum of mothering experiences. At last we are speaking out about the difficult, challenging, funny, thought-provoking, wonderful and sometimes tragic experiences of mothering our adolescent children. This anthology contains pieces in which women grit their teeth as they describe the wearing day-to-day battle of adolescence. It contains pieces written with irony and humour and admiration. There are wonderful poems capturing strong emotions. And there are tales of appalling sadness which moved me to tears. And so this book reaffirms that in some way each mother's experience of adolescence is unique, just as her relationship with her son or daughter is unique. Yet at the same time there are common threads, recurring themes and feelings which are reflected from piece to piece like so many mirrors.

Although it is impossible to rank women's experiences of the teenage years on some Richter scale, it seems to me reading these pieces of writing, and all the others that did not make the final selection, that when we talk about adolescence we are describing a huge continuum of behaviour. Some mothers, I suspect a minority, get off relatively lightly, perhaps because of some lucky mix of personalities or perhaps because their teenagers just do not rebel. There is no ghastly phase when for a while their children turn into monsters. Then there is the middle ground of what we might call typical or normal or ordinary adolescence, although it's hard to know where to draw its boundaries. This is the familiar stuff of door-slamming, scowling, filthy bedrooms, and emptied fridges which so many women wrote about. The accounts included here – in which the worst is over fairly quickly, and nothing too dreadful happens before the teenager starts to get out of bed before mid-day again — will be particularly empowering for many women who will recognise in them much of their own experience and be able to relish the humour and share the frustrations. But beyond this there are more painful pieces. Some mothers have not only gone through hell with their teenage children, but have had the courage to share their experiences with us, so that this anthology will bring comfort and support to parents who have had, or are experiencing, serious difficulties with their children, including illness, drug addiction or bereavement. To these women writers I can only express my admiration, sympathy and astonishment at their bravery.

Reading these pieces of writing, what strikes me most keenly is how very hard women are on themselves. Perhaps it is a reflection of the way women are still expected to be the copers and carers in our society, the ones who always pick up the pieces. I have strong images of women bending over backwards, turning themselves inside out, as they try and try to understand and accommodate the often impossible behaviour of their teenage children. These pieces are riddled with confessions of inadequacy, guilt, blame, and shame. Women hate themselves for not conforming to some ideal of the perfect mother, yet in the circumstances which they describe, under the pressures which they have to bear, in a society which offers little support and undervalues the contribution they make, how could anyone do better? One mother writes: 'I hated myself for all this.' Another: 'I feel bad about it. I feel crap.' We have such unreal, impossible expectations for ourselves: 'I want to be a mother who knocks up an economical quiche before breakfast, or bones fish for chowder.' Yes — and hold down a full-time job and keep an eye on the elderly mother and run round the supermarket while our teenage child lies in bed all day watching TV! So when our adolescent ends up at the police station, or becomes dependent on drugs, or runs away from home, we point the finger at ourselves. When we shout and cry and lie awake night after night and bite our nails until they bleed, we are horrified because we are doing the 'shameful opposite of what the text-books tell you to do.'

Women seem to have enormous difficulty portraying their teenage children in a bad light. Throughout this anthology, there are portraits of women doing their best, struggling, coping, picking up the wet towels and saying sorry while their big children behave like little shits. It is time to be kinder to ourselves. It is not always our fault.

Maybe I should have called this book *The Loneliness of the Long-Distance Mother* because I am left with an almost universal impression of isolation and lack of support as mothers try to cope with their children's teenage years. What seems to be so striking in this anthology is the lack of active male partners. Inevitably this has a lot to do with the way contributions were solicited and no doubt fathers have their own stories to tell. It would be good to hear them. But in the context of this anthology, fathers are missing. Or they are silent, not contributing, unengaged, and not participating. In a moving passage, Rosalind Brackenbury describes opening the door at 2 a.m., having called the police about her missing son, to find him on her doorstep. 'It's at times like these that I long for there to be someone else, someone calm, sane and helpful, who knows what to do; perhaps a calm, sane version of myself.' True, many of the pieces are written by single parents, reflecting the ratio of single-parent to dual-parent families in our society, but many of the women who have husbands or partners write as if they, too, are dealing with their teenagers on their own. Kate Bromfield writes: 'He lives in the same house as us, sits at the same meal table; mentally he is elsewhere ... In common with many women in a so-called "partnership" I feel as if I am bringing up my children alone.' And even when fathers are 'sharing' the upbringing of teenagers following separation, they get the 'bursts of jolly fatherhood', the treats and holidays, withdrawing when it suits them, while mothers are left with the daily grind of routine and discipline.

Many single parents do carry extra emotional baggage which is painful and self-critical. As several contributors to this anthology point out, it is always difficult to sort out the difference between 'normal' teenage problems and what is attributable to the difficulties of bringing up an adolescent on one's own. Of course none of us who have been in this position will ever know the answer. Our teenager might have been just as awful had the father remained under the same roof. But single mothers go on tormenting themselves with images of what might have been. I want to thank Maggie Woods for bursting this terrible bubble of single-parent responsibility and idealism so splendidly: 'With perfect mutually supportive parents, or the single mother who is not "inadequate", this boy would say "please" and "thank you", play the cello like Casals, shop and cook dinners twice a week, and be kind to old people and babies. Bullshit.'

Several women also refer to the lack or unhelpfulness of statutory professional help. When mothers are having difficulties with their teenage children, there often seems to be nowhere to turn.

I have included lots of pieces about daughters as well as sons, but the fact that submitted pieces about boys outnumbered pieces about girls by about six to one deserves comment. Why are sons so very difficult? In one of our support groups, one mother said that however stroppy and verbally nasty her daughter was, she still felt in control. With her son, she felt powerless. Some sons seem to wage a more physical war against their mothers. Reflecting the domination of men over women in society, they can be intimidating or treat their mothers like the proverbial doormat. Yet antler-locking is the wrong role for mothers, and to confront a large boy child is as 'appropriate as a butterfly attempting to befriend a bull-elephant'. It is not their fault. Faced with today's laddish culture, they soon get the message that it is not cool to be sensitive, gentle and caring. As well as being angry, we feel sad and sorry for them. And not all the pieces about sons are negative. Rosalind Brackenbury writes with enormous admiration and understanding about her disabled son's loud raging and uncompromising rejection of the glitzy eighties. Caeia March writes of her sons' acceptance of her coming out as a lesbian and of her chronic illness: 'Through anguish and turmoil they hung on in there, wanting more of me, needing to know me even when I continued to represent unsafety.' As mothers, our relationships with our sons are hugely complex, but daughters too cause their own kind of havoc. They are lippy, scathing and critical. They can go off the rails as dramatically as boys. Women have written accounts of daughters who have become drug addicts, vagrants, truants and in need of psychiatric care. And of course we worry that they won't feel positive about their bodies, menstruation, sexual experiences, being female. As we struggle with poverty and pointless part-time employment, we worry that we are not offering them the right role model. Lynne Smith speaks for many women when she says that she wants her daughter to be 'a free spirit', unfettered by the expectations of traditional female roles. And yet this young woman ends up absorbed 'in domesticity.'

Many women ask for answers to the problems that beset them as their children grow large and angst-ridden. Many more admit that probably there aren't any. Several have suggested that the only way to make sense of the turbulence which characterises this phase of our mothering is to think of our teenagers' tantrums as nest-leaving behaviour. It's all about separation, and it's basic biological stuff. Here are our children grown big, trying to know themselves, trying to separate from us, pushing away our protection because they know that very soon they will have to stand on their own two feet. And here we are, trying equally hard to let them go, wanting to give them their freedom and independence, but at the same time afraid for them because the world is not a comfortable place, and, despite what they may believe, they are still vulnerable.

One mother writes: 'He is my man–child. I know I must begin to let go.' And so adolescence is a time of violent, warring emotions. We clash. Our teenage children have to rebel against us in order to be themselves. We watch them make mistakes and try to warn them. They do not listen. We put up barriers for their own protection, but they tear them down. In their efforts to make the difficult transition from child to adult, they take on new guises and become the sort of people who, under any other circumstances, we would not allow over the doorstep. And into this cauldron of emotions we pour our mother love. We may no longer like our children, but we still love them. No wonder the writing in this anthology is coloured with the vocabulary of emotional violence, as Maggie Woods says: 'This book would not exist unless there were some almost universal problem which bedevils the relationship between mothers and their growing children. The closer you have been, the bloodier and more difficult the separation.'

This book is for mothers, about mothers. But it is also about teenagers. In these pages, there is an acknowledgement of what they, too, are going through. We understand the impact of hormones which make them oblivious of anyone's needs but their own. We understand the oppression of a society which no longer values our young people enough to invest in their education or their future. Our teenagers are not stupid; they know what they have inherited. Rosalind Brackenbury writes of: 'The war of the world against young, defenceless people, our children.' Our children worry about unemployment, pollution, inequality, cruelty, violence, and if the the odds seem stacked too high against them, they give up and drop out. And so, however exhausting their rebellion, we have to admire their ability to see through the complacency and hypocrisy. And while they may be street-wise they still need our support and protection. Again Rosalind Brackenbury: 'Your child knows the score better than you do and is a better bullshit detector by far. You'd better listen, you'd better learn, and you'd better get tough.' Describing her complex relationship with her own son she says: 'You pushed and shoved and fought me from complaining mother to radical accomplice . . . what you demanded of me was what every young person needs, an ally, someone to stick by you no matter what.'

There are sad endings to the teenage years recorded in this anthology as our sons and daughters walk out of our lives, or we send them off to try the greener grass with their fathers. There are tragic endings. There are happy endings. There is forgiveness, love, and somewhere a bunch of flowers. But above all else one senses relief, acceptance and resignation as we and our teenagers come out the other side. 'I still feel guilty about my relief that Sophie's gone,' writes Barbie Ordish, 'but can't deny it. And I can accept I'm not the perfect mother far better now I'm not living in the midst of a civil war.' Descriptions of the final days of mothering teenagers are littered with images and metaphors − of silver linings, and clouds parting, of sunlight streaming in, of the fires of transformation, and women breaking out of prisons. But whether we watch our adolescents finally emerge centred and calm, whether we rub along as best we can, weathering the ups and downs, or whether in the end we lose our children, there are no final endings because our mothering goes on. Jean Buffong writes: 'The battle is not over yet. As long as life goes on a battle is being fought, but we are living, living and winning.' And if we are very fortunate (and this has happened to me) the child who became a stranger at my table is slowly transformed again into a very dear friend.

Helen Braid

Love in a Lamb Chop

Diana Mason

There is a vortex in our kitchen. A deep, swirling pit that most of the time you wouldn't even notice.

Some psychologists say that adolescents shake the walls of the home to test the security provided for them, and that parents should tighten up on discipline. In my experience, stronger walls merely accelerate the ricochet effect of unstable adolescent power. I have smashed china and a SuperGlued phone to prove it. In a household containing adolescents, like glass containing a volatile liquid, the restraining walls are less important than the state of the contents.

In my stronger moments I can admit that I, too, am volatile. I can crash into rage or self-pity at a moment's notice.

Preparing meals strains mothering to the limit. I sneak a glance at the vortex and pick up my purse. Pushing a wire trolley forward and financial commonsense back, I spend far too much money in the supermarket. The eldest has hit a healthy eating patch. I pile bran flakes and yoghurt (plain) in the trolley, knowing it won't last. Next week he'll be back on the beefburgers and the bran flakes will go soft in the cupboard. No matter — *I listened*. I am aware. I hover over the cold meats. One likes corned beef, the other preaches white meat (he watched a documentary on heart attacks). I buy both, wincing at the cost.

Beneath the four-feet sign saying DRINKS there's still no easy formula. Health-food child wants real juice, no Es, but no sugar means the other one won't drink it. I buy both again. Trapped by anxiety I overspend.

By fresh meats I'm deeply depressed. The same arguments apply — healthy white meat versus fatty affordable. I go for the expensive. I want to be a mother who knocks up an economical quiche before breakfast, or bones fish for chowder. I reason that they wouldn't eat either anyway, and I slip a bottle of red wine down each child leg-hole in the trolley.

I go home and take to the kitchen, chopping and frying, drinking wine and breaking into a sweat. I want to nurture them. I *need* them to appreciate the effort I put into responding to their diet fads. I want them to realise that this means I'm striving to understand their worries. But they only eat, heads down, bickering.

Steam rises, windows cloud over. The vortex fizzes. I push for a compliment, some kind of sign that they've received love from me in a lamb chop. Noticing me, they criticise the gravy. I point out the time it takes to shop and cook; the money I spent on it all. They point out the wine I buy. They talk about their friends' mothers, the ones that stayed married and have two incomes. Harsh words are spoken and the vortex begins to rumble. I hear 'selfish', then 'whingeing' and 'pathetic'.

I chose to be alone. I closed the two-parent door for them, and denied them a choice. Their anger is real, born of incomprehension and frustration, and mine is compounded by guilt. Depression encourages me to picture them as orphans, exaggerating the ten-mile distance from their father in my mind until they are abandoned in a desert and I am responsible. There is a danger of tears. I may cry and truly earn 'pathetic'.

I recover, and snap and snarl. I tried to be a partner, and I put in my fifty per cent. The vortex rumbles and crackles, emitting sparks.

On bad days, resentment and fury cannot be contained. One insult leads to another, someone will hit a raw spot, and we will fly at each other. The vortex erupts. We get locked in the spin, faster and faster, until we are thrown apart, weary and hurting. Then we crawl away into our separate spaces, where we make phone calls or tune in the radio, reaching for the outside world.

The vortex settles back, churning and clicking.

Maria's Clothes

Helena Hinn

Maria's mother threw out Maria's clothes.

Maria returned home from town one afternoon to find that all her clothes had disappeared from her wardrobe. Gone were the workman's donkey jacket her mother had promised to dry clean and the navy dungarees, splattered with plaster, which Maria had thought were in the wash.

Outside, in the back yard, Maria found her mother standing over the dustbin. Triumphantly. And Maria, possessing only the clothes she stood up in, was taken to Debenhams by her mother who bought her a blue linen dress with a white flowered pattern.

As if her mother hoped that, by changing the clothes her daughter wore, she could change her daughter's personality into one she felt more suitable — that she preferred.

Travels with a Pram and Hot Flush and the Toy Boy

Sara Yeomans

The supper things squatted, unwashed and slimy, in the sink. Odd mugs and plates and knives and socks and topless jars of Bovite lay around the living room. My hackles rose. It was half past nine in the morning and the only thing that stirred was an inane television presenter who was shrieking and gesticulating and grimacing into my home. The telephone began to ring.

A dozing heap beneath the duvet in front of the telly heaved and reared up and turned into Jane. 'It's all right Mum, I'll get it. It's bound to be for me.' Bound to be, I thought. I tried not to listen, but intense words and phrases about relationships and subtexts kept breaking through the idiot presenter's squawks. My daughters spoke a different language from the one I used, in what, as they had once kindly explained to me, is the non-specific dialect of their age. It abolishes all consonants and runs together all remaining sounds into a singsong, upturned with a question mark at the end of each phrase. Its beauty, I was told, lies in the fact that it is completely free of any class or educational connotations. Its disadvantage, I once dared to say, is that it is also completely free of sense, logic and communication. Harriet and Jane retorted that a remark like that was a perfect example of my social and educational arrogance.

'Yeah, yeah, yeah', Jane was saying down the phone, just like the Beatles. 'Yeah. I dunno. Jowamean?'*

I switched on the hoover and pushed it angrily around the floor between the socks and plates and knives and topless jars. Mistake yapped when the postman shoved the letters through the door. I switched off the hoover and fell over her on the way to pick them up. 'Yeah, yeah, yeah,' said Jane again. 'It's the hidden agenda you've got to watch out for, jowamean?' Shag the hidden agenda, I thought, what about the washing up? I picked up the post. Electricity bill, house insurance reminder, television licence reminder, poll tax demand, telephone bill. Telephone bill. I stared at it, frozen into disbelief. One hundred and seventy-one pounds forty-three pence. It was impossible, it was a mistake. Mistake wagged her tail and looked adoringly at me, and I lashed out at her. According to this phone bill, towns and cities all over the country were linked by soundwaves all leading to my home. 'Yeah, yeah,' said Jane again. It was not a mistake, it was one hundred and seventy-one pounds forty-three pence worth of non-specific dialect conversations about subtexts and hidden agendas.

I spun round and seized the telephone from Jane's astonished hand. 'Enough,' I said.

She gazed at me in appalled disbelief. 'What the hell are you doing?'

'I'm banning the telephone. You and your classless subtextual friends will have to communicate by pigeon from now on.'

---

* 'Jowamean?' is non-specific dialect for, 'Do you know what I mean?'

Jane was pale with outrage. 'How dare you interrupt my private phone calls?'

I held out the phone bill in a shaking hand. 'This is how I dare. This is how. Who the bloody hell is going to pay for this lot? Have you got a hundred and seventy-one pounds forty-three pence to spare? Because I certainly haven't.'

Jane began to laugh in a superior, spiritual sort of way. 'For God's sake, Mum, it's only money. Life's about more than money, you know. Property is theft, jowamean?'

That did it. Years of trying to be nice to my children, of believing that if I loved them, if I treated them with courtesy and respect and kindness and generosity they would do the same for me, exploded in my face and I spanked Jane hard on her bottom. It was the first time in either of our lives that I had done it.

Her mouth fell open. 'You can't do that.'

I did it again, just to make sure. 'Now you listen to me for once,' I said. 'Just you sit down and listen to me.' There was no subtext here, just one furious woman and a telephone bill.

'Listen to me,' I said again. 'Our generation brought you lot up on a lot of child-rearing theories about the awful dangers of making you constipated and homosexual and depressed and repressed if we ever punished you or criticised you or in any way let you think that you were less than wonderful or deserved anything less than pure happiness. We praised your every word and action, we discussed politics and religion with you before we sat you on your potties, we never made you do anything you didn't want to do and we've reared a whole generation of arrogant spoiled brats with ludicrously inflated ideas about their own talents and importance who are utterly selfish, who shout about Third World human rights while they treat their own mothers like slaves and idiots. Well, this slave and idiot has had enough.' I slammed out of the house and caught the bus to Tarminster, where I realised two things. One was that Jane had been taking the phone call and not making it. The other was that I was still wearing my apron.

When I returned, I could hear Harriet talking on the far side of the front door. She was on the phone, describing my revolution to a friend. 'Of course,' she was saying, 'I could read her subtext clearly, jowamean? It's redirected anger. Yeah. Like overspill. Right. I mean it wasn't about the phone bill at all really, it was something far deeper than that, jowamean?'

I gritted my teeth, opened the front door and pushed past her into the kitchen. The pile of washing up was deeper than ever.

Tom

Jill Robinson

This story will be familiar to parents the length and breadth of the land. Tom was lovely at four, but it was then that I separated from his father. By the time he was fourteen I was unable to cope. I had the choice of keeping him, or handing him over to the other parent.

Throughout his teens, Tom criticised everything. He criticised the state of the house which he said he was ashamed to bring friends to. He criticised my car — an old Ford Escort — and asked to be dropped off at the top of the road rather than at the school gates. He even criticised my size (14), pointing out that our neighbour had had three children and that she was still lovely and slim. His father, in contrast to me, had a house with a fitted kitchen and a stylish car. Did these things really matter so much to Tom?

Tom resented me going into his room, which I did occasionally, running in with clean clothing or sheets, pausing only to round up the dirty underwear from the floor before dashing out again. When I desisted, at his request, I was told off for not providing a clean games kit, after he had failed to put his clothes in the dirty laundry basket. And what sort of a dreadful mother fails to ensure that her son has a fresh supply of socks . . .

He wanted £50 for trainers. Everyone else had them and nothing else would do. At that time I did not have £50 to spare, but by great good fortune I was contacted by the editor of a local magazine who urgently wanted an article after someone else had let them down. A thousand words. £50 payment on publication. I borrowed the money from the gas bill fund, wrote the article, and Tom bought his trainers. When he wanted a mountain bike, I sold an Art Deco vase which had belonged to my late mother.

When I fell ill with glandular fever, I asked Tom for help with the washing up.

'Why should I do it?'

'Because I'm not well.'

'Oh, you're always moaning about something. Anyway, I'm allergic to washing-up liquid.'

I made a mental note to start saving for a dishwasher.

I did not really believe that giving in on such matters was the right thing to do, but the alternative was a row, or sullen resentment which could go on for weeks. I explained that it would be better if he learnt the value of money by getting a paper round or a spare time job; that he should not regard me simply as a provider of food, clean linen and transport. I pointed out that people came in different shapes and sizes, and that some people actually liked size 14 women, even if he preferred pencil-slim waifs. I said that I had better, more interesting and important things to do than clean the house incessantly, such as earning a living and studying for a higher degree. And that with his room in such a state he was in no position to criticise.

Tom was intelligent, or so I was told by his school. I was articulate and reasonable. But we did not seem able to communicate. It was obvious that he did not love or respect me. Were all adolescents this selfish? Would he behave the same way if his father were present? Maybe I had tried to over-compensate for the split, as some of my friends had suggested.

Then, in the middle of an English lesson, Tom had what his worried teacher described as an epileptic fit. The doctor told him that his body was developing rapidly and that he was making too many demands of it. He was refusing to go to bed at an acceptable time and playing computer games until midnight. His mind was over-stimulated and he wasn't able to sleep. Go to bed earlier, the doctor said, don't play computer games late at night, and get up in time to eat a good breakfast. If I'd handed the GP a script he couldn't have echoed more completely the arguments I had been putting to Tom.

But Tom was unimpressed. He wouldn't listen to me and he wouldn't listen to the doctor. The only person he respected and admired was his father. So, at that point I decided to hand him over. The move could be made at the end of the school year when Tom would be embarking on his GCSE courses and could be settled for the next two years.

To my surprise, Tom would not go. He wanted to remain here, at the same school, with his friends, even, he said, with his little brother. He did not, of course, mention me. By that time, I really wanted him to go. My decision had been made. His father, being male, would be able to empathise with him better, and I felt so exhausted. But Tom would not go, and I relented.

Over the next two years things got worse. There were terrible arguments, and in their aftermath Tom would smash furniture, wrench cupboard doors off their hinges, take a rolling-pin to the plaster work, or break a window. I began to wonder if he were schizophrenic, but the GP did not think it was anything serious. Nor the vicar, who said he could remember smashing dinner plates himself during his own adolescence. He even suggested that there was a silver lining – at least I knew where Tom was. Yes, he was at home, smashing up the furniture. I wondered if I could be forgiven for wishing that he was out vandalising the bus shelter.

I needed help. I spoke to Tom's father who said that I must be provoking him. I told Tom's form teacher about my problems, but he looked embarrassed and changed the subject. I asked a senior social worker for advice but was told that under the Children's Act 1989 parents are responsible for their children, even if they are beyond control. It appears there is strong legislation to protect children, but precious little to protect parents.

My friends were shocked. Some reassured me that Tom's problematic behaviour would pass in time. Others simply said that they would not put up with it. I had no wish to put up with it. But what could I actually *do*? Hit him? The law frowns on corporal punishment, and anyway he was bigger and stronger than me. Stop his pocket money? Since receiving a small legacy from his grandmother, he no longer had any pocket money. Keep him in? He was *always* in.

Finally, after he had broken yet another piece of our furniture, and I had spent a tearful hour on the telephone to the Samaritans, my sorrow turned to anger. I told him that if he did it again, I would treat him like any other young hoodlum I caught damaging my property. I would report him to the police.

'And what would they do?'

I said that I was not sure, possibly interview him, perhaps caution him, but there was one certain way to find out. So far, we have not had to put this approach to the test.

Now aged sixteen, Tom's behaviour has quietened down, just as my kind and worried friends told me it would. Following a windfall recently, we went on holiday to Catalonia where Tom made elaborate sand sculptures on the beach and visited art galleries to admire the works of Picasso and Dali. I know he enjoyed the trip because on our return I overheard him on the phone describing it in animated detail to his father. Generally, Tom cannot bring himself to utter more than the odd monosyllable to me – but even this may be changing. We almost had a conversation recently about simultaneous equations. Tom had emerged from his room at about 11.30 p.m. with tears in his eyes to ask me if I could remember how to do them. The last time I was required to solve equations was when I took O level maths in 1967, but I dredged my memory and Tom was grateful and relieved.

Now the GCSEs are imminent, and the Glastonbury Festival follows. Tom and his friend George are planning to go, having bought their tickets and looked out their tent. Tom pays full fare on the trains, his national insurance number has arrived, and I have been asked to surrender his child benefit in the autumn if he does not take up a place at sixth-form college. He will even be able to vote in the next Election. He has changed from a nightmare son into a young man.

But bringing him up on my own has been the hardest thing I have ever done.

We've Only Just Begun!

Kate Bromfield

This week, as I begin thinking about this piece, it is International Women's Week. I should really, I suppose, be writing about my daughter who is sixteen, bright and beautiful and of whom I am incredibly proud. She is turning into the kind of young woman I always hoped she would become: thoughtful, affectionate, funny, free-thinking, independent. She deserves her own story to be told, but not now. I am going to write about Joe, my son.

Joe will not want me to write this. He will say that I am 'showing him up'. He has never been sure whether he likes to be the centre of attention. Emily has *always* known! Well, good for her! She'll say, 'It's not fair! You're always giving him more of your time, your attention, your affection, your money,' etc. Basically, I can't win. I do my best to answer the needs of both of them as far as I can but there are times when the balance is *unequal* and they have to accept that. So, *tough*, Emily. And *tough*, Joe — whether you like it or not, this is about you.

There is a two-year-and-two-month age gap between my two children, and Joe is the youngest. I had always wanted at least three children but I have MS and a minor heart problem and was advised to stop with two. They are very precious.

Joe is fourteen. His voice has deepened and his feet are large. He is over six feet tall and very slender. He is one of the tallest in his year at school and says that he feels like Canary Wharf in assemblies. He needs constant reassurance that he is not freakish. I like his height; now he can rest *his* chin on *my* head when he is feeling affectionate. I cherish these moments, they are becoming increasingly rare. He is my man-child. I know I must begin to let go.

Joe's father has already let go. He lives in the same house as us, sits at the same meal table; mentally he is elsewhere. I am not sure that he means it to be like this but he is immersed in his work. In common with many women in a so-called 'partnership' I often feel as if I am bringing up my children alone. There have been times when I have virtually given up trying to communicate with my husband and we live almost entirely separate lives. I am aware that we are providing the children with a very poor role model as far as adult relationships are concerned but I've done my best and I can't do any more. I've had enough.

Joe, as yet, hasn't quite had enough. I watch him trying to relate to his father and frequently being met with either a complete lack of response, or irritation or downright hostility. Joe is so desperate for reaction that he goes too far; he becomes rude, he refuses to give up on a joke. If he initiates a play fight he doesn't know when to stop. He has a long way to go before he is as strong as his father either emotionally or physically. I try not to interfere. It's not easy.

Joe, at fourteen, is still gentle, sensitive, very aware of other people's needs. He is not a wimp but he is definitely not macho man. He makes us laugh with his imitation of the 'rude-boy' swagger, with his tongue-in-cheek adoption of city slang. He is intelligent, witty, aware of the pressures he is under to conform. He is learning to play electric guitar, is interested in all types of rock music. He wears mainly black denim and faded T-shirts with black trainers or baseball boots. His friend Chris is into heavy metal music, has below shoulder length hair and a black leather jacket covered with studs. 'You look so boring Joe,' he says. 'You're going to have to do something.' Joe's friend Fred, however, has a different look. He combs his short hair forward into a solid fringe and thinks that Joe should do the same. As Joe plays the guitar with Fred and Chris at different times and they each want to form a band which includes Joe, he is in a dilemma. But his hair has decided for him – it is thick and curly and has a will of its own. If he tries to grow it he looks like a Rubens' cherub or, if he tries to flatten it, he looks like Walter the Softie in the *Beano*. So he has it shaved at the bottom and short on the top. And we can't afford to buy him a leather jacket anyway.

I had expected Joe to be self-conscious about his looks. I was not surprised when the child who had been quite happy to run around nude began to close the shower-room door and to clutch the bath towel very tightly to him if we should catch him unawares. I was prepared, too, for his increasing moodiness and apparent need to spend hours up in his bedroom by himself. Although I did not like it much, it seemed like normal teenage behaviour.

We have been attending a cardio-thoracic outpatients clinic since Joe was eleven. The bones on the right side of his chest have been developing differently from the left side since birth and he was being monitored. We knew that he might possibly need an operation once he stopped growing but that certainly wasn't something that I thought about all the time. I was more caught up in day-to-day living. Now, looking back, I think I must have shelved the problem, put it to the back of my mind.

There was a short period of time last summer when the weather was very hot. I noticed that Joe continued to wear his school T-shirt, sweatshirt and jacket even when temperatures reached into the 80s, but other than nagging or teasing him occasionally, I didn't take much notice. Other adolescent boys either stripped off their tops at every opportunity, or shrouded themselves in as many layers as possible.

Then, one evening last summer, Joe called me from the shower. 'Mum! When are we going to the hospital again?' His voice was shaking slightly and I went in to him. It was so long since I had seen him naked. It was like seeing a stranger. I hadn't realised that he had pubic hair. I hadn't realised he was so thin. One side of his chest looked as if it had turned in on itself; where the ribcage should have protruded was a hollow. He could have rested a football in it without it rolling away.

I realised that Joe must have been watching this change for months. Alone. I felt I had failed him.

We saw the consultant at the beginning of August and he had his operation on October 7th. All his ribs had to be broken and two metal bars inserted behind them to push out the chest wall.

On the morning of the operation Joe's father and I were allowed to go with him down to theatre, walking quickly behind his trolley as he was wheeled down endless empty corridors, through heavy doors which thwacked shut behind us. We suddenly entered a room where the light seemed very bright, like walking from the wings onto a spotlit stage. People wore gowns and their heads were covered. Someone, the anaesthetist, stepped forward and Joe was given an injection. He turned his head and grinned at me mischievously, sending up the situation, 'Goodbye, Mum!' He closed his eyes – a tear rolled down his cheek. He was immediately surrounded by people and wheeled away. He was no longer ours. 'Is that it?' I said. 'That's it,' someone answered and laughed. We were ushered out.

I stood in the corridor outside and started to cry. 'Why did he say goodbye like that? Stupid boy. It's just not funny.' I wanted to begin all over again. I didn't feel ready.

We were told that the operation would probably take several

hours, that it would be a good idea if we went to have some breakfast before we returned to the ward. We would be contacted as soon as Joe came round from the anaesthetic and we could go down to the recovery room to be with him. It was eight o'clock in the morning. We sat in an 'Upper Crust' on the station near the hospital, drank coffee and watched people going to work and the pigeons scuffling underneath their feet. My husband talked about his work and football and did the crossword puzzle in the paper, his way of coping I think. I found it difficult to think of anything except what was going on in the operating theatre. I don't think I spoke at all. We went back to the hospital and sat almost in silence for another three hours.

The nurse in the recovery room told me that the first thing he did when he came round was yell my name. I didn't recognise him at first, he looked like a much younger child, a very small dark head at the end of an expanse of white blanket. One of his lungs had collapsed during the operation and he had an oxygen mask over his face. It seemed to me that he had tubes and drips and bottles everywhere. I managed to find a finger to hold.

I think when you're thirteen often your only reference point for 'hurt' is that which you have already experienced and Joe's young life had been virtually pain free. Now he was in agony, shut inside himself, focused on the pain. He was confused and frightened by the drips, by the clip attached to his finger, by the bottle attached to his side into which blood was draining. He was desperate to pee but he wouldn't use a bottle, was too inhibited to let the nurse hold it for him and wouldn't let us help him either.

The first afternoon after the operation seemed to set a pattern for the remainder of his recovery period. The slightest movement in the bed was excruciating for Joe so, although he complained about being uncomfortable, he wouldn't move at all unless he had a nurse to supervise him. Now I wonder whether he thought the operation had gone wrong because he had not been prepared for so much pain. Maybe he thought that his ribs might separate again if he moved. I tried to talk to him about what he was thinking but he wouldn't, maybe couldn't, say.

Joe was so disorientated by the pain, the drugs, the number of different professionals with whom he had to deal that he simply shut us all out. The hospital staff were brilliant but he would not respond to them, to me or to his dad. He refused to co-operate, would not attempt the physiotherapy exercises he was given, refused to eat the hospital food. I was desperate. Why couldn't he realise that in order to get stronger he had to help himself? I was exhausted both emotionally and physically and so anxious that I became impatient and angry with him, when I knew I should be strong and supportive. I was at a complete loss to know how best to deal with him. What I really wanted to do was hug him tightly and say, 'It's okay, you'll get through this,' but there were dark, irrational times when I began to doubt it and the drips and the drugs and Joe's scarred chest created more than just a physical barrier between us.

During his postoperative period at home we became locked in a miserable battle of wills. I had to force him to do things in order to recover. If he managed to get himself into a comfortable position he would refuse to move and it was a temptation for me to do things for him, but I knew I had to make him get up, move around, wash, dress, sit at a table to eat. He had been told at the hospital that if he held a cushion to his chest it could help to relieve the pain and he carried it round with him everywhere. It was painful for him to move his arms freely to use a knife and fork and it was, of course, impossible if he tried to hold the cushion too! Now we can laugh. At the time it was one more frustration.

He had been told that he had to take exercise in order to strengthen his lungs. I persuaded him to accompany me on walks round the block. Sometimes it could take a whole morning for him to get himself ready. I used to wait downstairs in the kitchen trying to keep a little bit to my old routine, trying to write, not being able to concentrate, knowing that he was upstairs sitting on his bed plucking up the courage to move. I knew he was in pain; we both were! We screamed at each other and loathed each other. We both like our own space and we were forced to be together too much of the time. He was so depressed that I wasn't happy about leaving him in the house on his own. I was very unsure of his mental state. He said, frequently, 'This hasn't been worth it, Mum.' The day that he managed to walk down to the corner shop and back by himself liberated us both.

As I write this Joe has been back at school for five months. He has been involved in a fight. He has been mugged. He has watched a friend get picked up for shoplifting. Some of his peers have already begun to experiment with drink, drugs, sex. He is level-headed and aware. I hope he will remain so. That's the best I can do, I suppose: suggest caution and hope! Next school year, Joe wants to go skiing. The hospital registrar said on Monday, 'Yes, that's fine, but you must be careful not to fall on your chest.' Joe is a beginner. Help! Wish us both luck.

There Is No Such Thing as a Bad Boy; Only a Bad Mother

Maggie Woods

I have two sons. They are now 20 and 23. I have brought them up on my own for 16 years and it has been a bumpy ride. My marriage ended disastrously, with my ex-husband in a ferment of fury, determined to do nothing that might make life easy for us. So, until my younger son could go to school and for quite some time after, we existed on his divorce settlement of £50 per week, Oxfam clothes, beans, and terror of bills. The boys went to the local comprehensive as soon as they were old enough. I did the kind of ill-paid jobs that a Cambridge graduate can do when she is mother and father to two children, caught in a throttling money-trap with no money or support — interviewer for the Manpower Services Commission Jobshop, picture researcher for a part-work company, sub-editor and finally, writer.

My elder son, Paul, took on a heart-breaking weight of responsibility. My younger son, Kit, dwindled away until it was brought to my notice that at school he was attending classes for English as a second language. We muddled through five years or so of traumatic poverty and misery, which dented all of us. I behaved exactly as one should not – totally inconsistently. I was miserable and self-obsessed one minute, frantic, panicked and screaming about irrelevant trivia the next. Sometimes I stayed out late and got drunk, in a blind effort to have some kind of adult life. I told Paul that I longed to leave them both, to run away, that they had ruined my life. That kind of thing. The frantic and shameful opposite of what the text-books tell you to do.

I hated myself for all this, as well I should. I bit and picked at the cuticles of my nails until they bled, took up with a series of tediously tight-fisted men, and smoked heavily as part of a splendid repertoire of self-destructive habits. But in hindsight I was a tryer, floundering desperately out of my depth. As my succinct American friend Sharon said: 'When a marriage breaks up, parents should either put in time or money.' My ex-husband, myopically grudge-bearing, did neither. He festered away in his horrible flat feeling sorry for himself. An architect, he had lost his job two years before we separated, and he was damned if he would go out and get paid work of any other kind. So I laboured, took any job that came, worked overtime, and neglected my boys. At weekends, all I wanted to do was sleep. Preferably forever. They brought each other up, and became accustomed to the ever-radiant television as their most dependable source of warmth.

We were very loving too, and there were lots of cuddles. I read to them most nights and sang them to sleep until they found that too embarrassing. Weekends were a great pleasure, and we breakfasted on pancakes and maple syrup amid a welter of newspapers. I look back on that time as an agonised muddle, and can remember very little, and little of that without shame.

It was suggested that we undergo family therapy or counselling. My ex-husband refused to go, it was decided that Paul did not need it, so Kit and I signed up for several times a week for years. This was a curious exercise, and I do not really know if it achieved anything. I know for certain that the child psychotherapist whom I saw was not on my side. 'You will always find someone to punish you,' were his final words to me, sounding distinctly like a curse. Kit is still very puzzled by the instructions and questions of the woman whom he talked to. Possibly, helped by therapy, he will be a good, loving and understanding man one day. Right now he is more interested in misbehaving.

We jogged along until Paul hit 14. With some trepidation and treading a fearful financial tightrope I bought a house large enough to accommodate my sons and their friends, with a small football pitch of a garden in which we barbecued on summer evenings. I pushed the boat out for birthdays and Christmases although, to my lasting regret, we could never afford family holidays. For a while we were amicable, close, and humorous, and the boys got on very well with my friends and two of the more humane serial men in my life. Problems started when I fell in love with the — in most ways eminently suitable — man with whom I am still involved. He has children of his own and found it impossible to make room in his life for mine. A handful of serious relationships ended on me, but nothing hit me with quite the ice-cold shock of Paul's announcement one weekend that he would not always be around, and that he would probably be with his friends most weekends henceforward. Paul had taken on so much — looking after Kit, helping round the house. I realised I had come to depend on him rather than the other way around. I was shattered. Why did he want to leave and how would I cope?

Little by little cracks appeared in our affection for each other. He stayed out later and later. He did not look after Kit any more. They began to fight and apparently to dislike each other, which made Kit very lonely. We all became very embarrassed about physical contact, and the kisses and hugs that had been a natural reminder that, despite our rocky road, we were all right, suddenly became awkward and began to dwindle away. Paul began to smoke, stopped working, failed exams and, I see in retrospect, grappled with corrosive self-doubt and anger. He was in hell, and did not wish to be there alone. So we battled and hated together.

Bringing up boys requires Herculean strength of character and sense of right and purpose. It always comes as a shock quite how destructive a large boy can be without even registering his wake of chaos. How vigorously he will fight to defend his right to make a mess and do nothing to rectify it. What energy will go into outraged accusations of nagging. What otherwise untapped intelligence can be brought into play to prove that you are the one who is at fault. What potentially beneficial intuition is used to increase your guilt load.

I found myself on countless occasions trying to persuade, nag, coerce, blackmail, bribe, sometimes even terrorise my elder son into performing some token household task. I was fatally undermined by my guilty knowledge that I had not given the boys the good life I intended for them and they deserved – a seam of weakness Paul exploited ruthlessly. And in him I found an adversary that had me beat. We would simply lock horns and shout. Occasionally I was reduced to stamping my feet and screaming. Nothing changed. He would continue not to wash up, and I would continue to hate him for it. We would both feel aggrieved and slink off to our lairs, each cursing the other.

If you examine this situation as a mother, it presents a tangle of paralysing complexity. If you take it apart strand by strand – a painful exercise – you may find obvious threads, and recognisable knots and snarls. You will see your own guilt as a constant snare. You will find your child's rage and anger, his fear of your strength and your weakness, and above all his fear of the possibility that he may have caused all your problems and unhappiness. You will see his love for you, and his disappointment that you are not steady and dependable like Keith and Felicity. And you will know your love for him, and your disappointment that he is not glibly charming and cocky like Dan. You wish you could protect him from yourself, and yourself from him. You wish you could take back the absolutely unforgivable and APPALLING things you have said. And above all you wish that you did not cast this wicked spell on each other that leaves you both so stumped and bilious. In that moment when your reasonable request for help has been ignored just once too often, the carping voice that sneers at you: 'Have you never ignored your boys' needs?', will simply increase your own sense of impotence and rage. Guilt and self-criticism are no allies for the single mother. The object in the long run is not to be reasonable, or even honest, but to be effective.

Doberman owners like to come up with the complacent dictum: 'There is no such thing as a bad dog, only a bad owner.' Every mother of a recalcitrant adolescent boy will feel this as a dagger to the heart. We all suspect it to be true – with the right patient understanding and love, with time and listening, with an unassailable moral structure and an undentable sense of what is right, with the constant strength and vigilance to enforce your few wise rules and mean what you say, this belligerent boy would not be this way. With perfect mutually supportive parents, or the single mother who is not 'inadequate' this boy would say 'please' and 'thank you', play the cello like Casals, shop and cook dinner twice a week, and be kind to old people and babies.

Bullshit.

Rather than regret the fictional perfect son of a perfect parent (definition: not you), it is more useful to use as your guide the assumption that most boys still live in the jungle. Their path through adolescence is one of ducking and diving, of taking and exploiting. Of emptying the fridge, eating all the olives, and marking their territory by leaving dirty plates and socks in the sitting room. Or, if you are unlucky, by hiding their cigarette butts under the sofa, so that every particle of your home is thoroughly and permanently marinaded in the odour of Walthamstow pub. Of scenting their quarry and capturing their prey.

Few adolescent boys living at home think beyond their next spliff, drink, girl, football match, television programme or fight. Few boys living with their mother hear her at all. When testosterone is raging in the veins (or wherever it rages), a mother is absolutely surplus to requirements. With an adolescent boy, you are dealing with a different species, and all the sensitive nuances that make interacting with friends such a pleasure, are completely irrelevant and a severe handicap. Boys are simply walking chemistry, boiling with resentment and acne, farting noxious gases, exuding feet and armpits, and looking for a congenial place to put their dicks. Until these chemicals have run their course, and taken on some definition and predictability, your sensitive agonising about how to make him happy and fulfilled and interested in his A levels is as auspicious and appropriate as a butterfly attempting to befriend a bull-elephant.

The key is territory. This lumbering explosives factory is in your territory. Among animals, adolescent males get pushed out of home before they start trying to biff their fathers and mate with their mums. I suspect that this is just too obvious for most mothers to see. Too crude. And yet, this book would not exist unless there were some almost universal problem that bedevils the relationship between mothers and their growing children. The closer you have been, the bloodier and more difficult the separation.

I can admit all these terrible things because after nine years of pain too complex to cure and too painful to acknowledge, the clouds have parted and the sunlight is streaming down. Paul left home to go to college, where he met a girl who seems warm and tough and determined. She has induced him to get a job, to give up smoking, and to work hard at his course. He has taken hold of his life, seen the point of it, and no longer expends his energies blaming me. At the age of 51 I have rediscovered my own youth and joy in life. I have realised quite how heavy was the burden of his unhappiness and my impotence, and the exhilaration of losing it is all the greater for the contrast.

If I have hardly spoken of my younger son with whom I find myself in a state of perennial warfare about smoking and socks and staying out all night, it is because I now realise that the journey in the dark is bearable if you have evidence of light at the end. I am no angel, neither is Kit, but one day we will meet as adults, free of all the habits of bitterness. Paul and I talk to each other now, and, more astounding, listen to each other. He is a beautiful fellow and I feel very proud of him and love his company. After the years of mutual distrust he has merged with the completely loving and entirely lovable boy I once knew, before the poison of adolescence turned us both into monsters. A friend of mine once said: 'It's tough having a difficult 17-year-old. Wait until you have a difficult 47-year-old.' I am sure she is right, and that there will be horrible times to come when we will turn back into mad caricatures of mother and son. But the weight that has lifted is the curse of unalterable destiny. We are not definitively programmed or genetically determined. Paul has been able to break out of his adolescent prison and has liberated me. There were times when I was so miserable that I really thought that dying would be the better option. I am so very, very glad that I did not, and am still around to adore my son again. Unequivocally.

Sweet Sixteen

Barbie Ordish

MONDAY 13th

Went to Sainsbury's straight from work thinking I was being clever avoiding the peak-time queues. Discovered I was wrong (does nobody shop at normal times now?). Spent £87.63 on a few bits and pieces, got home knackered at 8.20 p.m. Sophie and Tessa protested it wasn't fair they had to help me carry the shopping from the car – they were tired and, besides, they were watching a really good film. Blew my top, threatened to chuck the TV out of the window. Sophie said, Fine, she'd just go and watch it at her boyfriend's. Ricky has his own telly and *his* mum doesn't nag all the time. Tessa scurried about, putting things away, offering to cook dinner, trying to diffuse the impending argument. Too weary for yet another confrontation, didn't even mention the pile of washing-up left from yesterday.

TUESDAY 14th

Got home at 6.35 p.m. Hordes of Sophie's friends and still the same dirty dishes. Tessa said she was about to do them. I replied how coincidental; she got huffy and flounced out of the kitchen. Started on the washing-up. Sophie breezed in, informed me Martin had phoned to say he'd no money for me this week and, by the way, could Ricky stay for a few days as he'd had a huge row with his mum. Muttered about Martin not caring if his daughters starved. And if I couldn't afford to feed two ravenous teenagers why should I object to a third? Sophie said it was my fault her dad had no money, I should have thought of that when I kicked him out. And if Ricky couldn't stay with us he'd end up in a shop doorway. Phoned Marie to check the situation. Apparently Ricky had stormed out this morning when she found out he'd not been to school for 3 weeks. She'd be happier knowing where he was, if I didn't mind. Said okay. Told Sophie it was on the condition that she didn't start bunking off too. She was amazed I even mentioned it; how could I imagine she'd be that stupid? Managed to keep my mouth shut.

Started thinking about Sophie and Ricky after they'd gone to bed. They've been together for 7 months – a long-term relationship at their age. I'd be naive to presume Sophie's still a virgin. But she's much more mature than I was at 16. And at least she's got someone who cares to share her first sexual experiences with. My initiation was in a converted double-decker bus and about as memorable as a McDonalds'.

WEDNESDAY 15th

Had to fight my way between bicycles to reach the front door. Found the kitchen vandalised. Only one egg and an empty margarine tub in the fridge and no bread. Sophie couldn't understand what all the fuss was about; Marie never minded Ricky's friends having a snack. Anyway, she'd clear up the mess later and couldn't we get more food at the corner shop? Instead of murdering her, yelled and threatened to throw everyone out if they weren't gone in two minutes. Sophie said not to worry, the whole street had probably heard me anyway and evacuated.

WEDNESDAY 22nd

Phone bill arrived as I left for work. Nearly a hundred and thirty pounds, despite my economy lectures. But a glimmer of hope – from now on I can have *every* call itemised. Their 'ring-off before 10 units then call back' trick won't work any more.

Sophie hoovering the stairs when I got home. Ricky had gone to talk to his mum. Tessa was at drama. Remarked what strange effects boredom had. Sophie got indignant, asked why I never appreciated what she did. Recognising a truce I apologised and we talked, 'woman-to-woman'. She asked me what I thought about the Pill. Told her it was a good idea if you weren't sleeping around. She said she'd got an appointment at the Family Planning Clinic. Gave her some boring advice about the dangers of AIDS, etc., which she endured patiently. Funny how, as a mother, you feel obliged to repeat stuff they know already. We discussed careers and what she wants to do. She hasn't a clue but has accepted the wisdom of A levels – more than I did at her age. And she promised to put more effort into her school work. Then Ricky arrived to say he was moving back to his mum's.

THURSDAY 23rd

Went to work late today so was still at home when Sophie left for school. Noticed she was wearing a clingy evening top. Became suspicious. Phoned the school, discovered she'd been absent all week. So much for not being 'that stupid'. Had an almighty row with her this evening, but not because I laid into her. I'd thought about it all day, decided more would be achieved if I talked to her calmly. She was furious I'd 'dared to check up' on her. Shouted abuse at me, marched off to visit her dad because 'he knows what it's like living with a control-freak.' Phoned Martin to tell him she was on her way. Ranted at him to let me know the outcome instead of provoking my 'them against me' paranoia with his usual wall of silence.

Tessa was torn between her concern for me, loyalty to her big sister, and her need to tell me her trainers are falling apart. She compromised by asking to spend the night at a friend's and left a note about her shoes. I was in bed by the time Sophie returned.

THURSDAY 2nd

Terrible atmosphere since the bunking-off episode. Sophie goes for revision lessons with Martin most evenings – his well-intentioned way of helping the situation. I'm tolerated with disdain. Don't even bother asking her to do anything around the house – 'Dad doesn't treat us like servants.' For Tessa's sake I side-step potential arguments. It's like shadow-boxing with a jelly fish. My survival technique is going out more often. And clutching onto the belief that 'this, too, will pass.' Keep reminding myself how awful I was at 16.

TUESDAY 7th

Let my resolve slip and had a go at Sophie this evening. She'd been on the phone since I got home. Didn't say anything, even when she demanded I turn the radio down. Then Margery called to say she's back from Australia. Been talking for a couple of minutes, Sophie started stomping around, complaining she was expecting an important call. That did it. Tessa's the innocent victim again, though. I've banned them both from using the phone. Locked it in my filing cabinet before going to bed.

THURSDAY 9th

Came home early, caught Sophie unplugging a 'spare' phone she'd got from Ricky. Then found three of her friends lounging on my bed watching TV because I'd been 'too lazy' to return it to her room. Apparently I'm the only mother in the world who doesn't provide full, *en suite* recreational facilities plus limitless use of telephone. And the fact that I once spent fifteen quid on a tube of make-up proves how selfish and greedy I am. Seriously considered running away from home but decided the dogs would miss me.

FRIDAY 10th

Telephone call from Rachel's mum. The usual social-worker babble; Rachel had told her things 'aren't going too well' between me and Sophie, would I like to talk about it? Replied, No thank you, I have friends to talk to. She said, Of course, but it's 'more beneficial to discuss problems of this nature with people less involved.' And Sophie's 'such a lovely girl', it's a shame we couldn't discuss matters like she and Rachel do.

SUNDAY 12th

Weekend of soul-searching. Stayed in to try and make amends with Sophie. Tearful, she accused me of never leaving her alone, then went to stay at Ricky's. Tessa got annoyed about us 'acting like stupid kids', went off to visit Martin. Watched a programme about how to cope with the 'natural' fear of losing one's children once they grow up. Decided there must be something wrong with me.

MONDAY 13th

Sophie promised to be home by 10 p.m., strolled in at 11.35. Didn't she know I'd wanted an early night, I snapped. She said if I didn't spend all my time going out having fun I wouldn't need one. Then she added that everyone feels sorry for her because I'm so cruel. And they pity Martin having to give me all his money to fritter in pubs. That's when I slapped her across the face. Told her to go and live with her bloody father if he was so wonderful. Her screams woke Tessa, who got frightened and burst into tears. The dogs panicked, started barking. Sophie grabbed her jacket and ran out of the door. Marie rang a few minutes later, said Sophie had just called from a phone box. Ricky was on his way to meet her and take her to Martin's. Went to sleep marvelling at how my mother had survived my nightmare years without me noticing a thing.

TUESDAY 14th

Phoned Martin, he said Sophie was too distressed to talk tonight. He'll bring her round tomorrow evening.

FRIDAY 17th

Sophie has gone to live with her father. I apologised for hitting her but she said she'll never forgive me. She's happier there; I made her life hell.

WEDNESDAY 22nd

Tessa came back from visiting Martin and Sophie, caught me crying. She did her 'little mother' act, tried to cheer me up. Told her I was sorry for her sake as much as any one's. She and Sophie have always been close and I know they'll miss each other. Tessa said, Yes, but we'll all be happier this way. She was fed up with the arguments and now her dad won't be so lonely with Sophie there. I hadn't thought of that – such wisdom from a thirteen-year-old.

FRIDAY 31st

Still feel guilty about my relief that Sophie's gone, but can't deny it. And I can accept I'm not the perfect mother far better now I'm not living in the midst of a civil war. My relationship with Martin has improved too; since we've got one daughter each (and his costs twice as much to run) I don't have to ask him for money. And now I can spend time with Tessa without snapping her head off. Perhaps there'll be problems with her later, but hopefully not for a couple of years. Maybe by then Sophie will have stopped seeing me as The Enemy.

FRIDAY 21st

Heard from Tessa that Sophie and Ricky split up last weekend and Sophie's heartbroken. Phoned her, she agreed to come out with me for a meal. She couldn't tell me about Ricky without crying, but we talked though she still kept her distance. Asked if she'd like to move back with me, she said we'd only start arguing again. And besides, her old room would remind her too much of Ricky. At least I've succeeded in producing diplomatic children.

MONDAY 24th

Went to work feeling more relaxed than for ages, now that Sophie's stopped ignoring me. Then I got a phone call. It was a man's voice. Did I have a daughter called Tessa? Bustle and noise in the background – hospital sort-of sounds. I panicked. There was no school today. Tessa had gone shopping in the West End with a friend. I pictured her crumpled body in the road, under a bus, battered and unconscious. Then the man said he was a security guard at the Body Shop in Oxford Street. Tessa had been caught shoplifting. Two eyeliners and a jar of lip-gloss. Don't suppose he thought much of me as a mother when I answered, 'Oh, is that all?'

To My Daughter

Pamela Lewis

What is there about the threshold?
There is no need to stand on it —
it is pleasant on both sides,
it is warm outside on a summer night
and you belong inside.

You linger on the grey stone step
two steps wide, an air lock
between hello and goodbye.
This is standing still
progression, and it takes hours.

I held your hand for many years
when we crossed the road.
Now you go out by yourself;
how long you wait on the doorstep
is entirely your own choice.

Fool's Gold

Jane Allan

When John was six, his father and I called it a day and separated. For the next five years we lived three minutes walk away from each other and managed to share (albeit unequally) the upbringing of our, by then, two boys.

The end of the marriage was also the end of the seething resentment and deep unhappiness which had eroded my self-esteem and rendered me constantly bad-tempered and miserable. Everything was working out well. I had a part-time job which allowed me to keep a roof over our heads, run a car, enjoy a reasonable life and be there for the children before and after school. The boys adapted well, spending the weekends with their father while I spent mine with a splendidly unsuitable lover. With space and time I was a much nicer Mummy – far closer to the idea of the mother I had always thought I would be. Money was tight – the boys' father, freed from the shackles of marriage and responsibility, had given up work and embarked upon a four-year university course. A self-professed new-man and caring father, he had the maintenance order suspended without a qualm – a degree in American studies would equip him for a better career which would benefit the boys. Did I say that the seething resentment had come to an end? While he wrote essays at leisure, I worked, looked after the boys, took in a lodger and embarked on an Open University degree course. Not for us mothers the luxury of abandoning all responsibilities to indulge an intellectual whim.

After five years the unsuitable lover had passed his sell-by date. A younger and more suitable lover appeared offering stability, security and a 'normal' family life which, after five years of single parenthood and an increasingly painful relationship, I had come to desire above everything else. There was one slight problem. I wanted that 'normal' family life, but could I leave my job, my house, my friends and lose my independence? The new man lived four hundred miles away in rural Scotland.

The boys were all for it. They liked James. Scotland seemed an exciting place to live. I agonised, consulted friends, parents, anyone who would listen. Should I? Shouldn't I? 'Yes, go for it,' they all cried in unison. The boys' father was less impressed. It had been okay for him to consider moving to America and France, but a move to Scotland for me was unthinkable. He liked things as they were – I had all the responsibility, he had easy access to the boys when he chose. In the end it was the eleven-year-old John who said 'You can't spend the rest of your life doing nothing just in case it doesn't work out.'

The boys settled well into their new school and new way of life. Their father had been there for them physically, but emotionally and intellectually he was too busy soaking up the academic life to pay them any real attention or mend bikes or take them swimming. There had been occasional bursts of jolly fatherhood which seemed to coincide with the appearance of new women in his life. What better accessory for a right-on, feminist man than his two sons? Especially when they live with their mother for most of the week.

Life seemed to be working out well. And then we hit adolescence.

The five years of part-time parenting had suited me well and I found the return to full-time motherhood quite a shock to the system. Coping with a new lifestyle and being in a full-time partnership had its inevitable difficulties. James did his best with the boys but he wasn't their dad so I had to bear the brunt of any aggro that flew about.

Adolescent boys soon weary of rural idylls. With a teenager's astonishing talent for boredom, life in the country has to be the pits. The five weeks a year spent with their father – the boys on best behaviour and dad throwing in a few treats – offered a more enticing vision of life than the one they had here. He was Nice Daddy at a Distance – good on rhetoric, completely crap at any real commitment, while I became Horrid Mummy who nagged about teeth-cleaning, homework and bedroom tidying and who always sussed out the lies and the stealing which had become a fairly major part of John's life.

John's father told lies and stole. To see these undesirable character traits coming out in John was unbearable. Despite spending very little time together, John's mannerisms, speech and demeanour became more and more like his father's. All the things I had grown to despise and detest in Derek were now manifesting themselves in my son. Money started disappearing. We were sure that John was responsible, but he would never own up so both he and his younger brother would be punished. Wallets and purses had to be locked away. I tried to explain how hurtful it was that someone in my own family would steal from me. Nothing I said had any effect. We thought that perhaps we were not generous enough and tried to give him more. Still money disappeared. The more he took, the less we wanted to give. We became grudging and resentful. As well as money, other items disappeared. Pens were a favourite, but only expensive ones; penknives; tapes; CDs. If it was small and portable, it was fair game. Special treats such as chocolate, biscuits or crisps bought for sharing would vanish. He even took his baby brother's Easter eggs. He would swear blind it wasn't him and yet took no trouble to hide the wrappers which spilled out of his pockets and littered his bedroom floor. If John wanted more from us he was going the wrong way about it.

It's hard to admit that you don't like one of your own children and even harder to live with it. The more like his father he became, the more difficult I found it to be warm and affectionate towards him and so we embarked on a downward spiral of constant confrontation and anger: arguments, door slamming, threats to leave home for an imagined wonderful life with his dad, and a general atmosphere of bad temper and unpleasantness.

Of course it wasn't all awful. I had rashly become pregnant and produced a third son. John loved his new baby brother and showed him all the affection that was lacking between us. Rather than an embarrassment – the embodiment of his ageing mother's sexuality – Thomas was quite a status symbol among John's mates. For a little while our new family seemed to gel and we were probably all as happy as we could have hoped to be.

Life was hectic and money tight during the winter of 1993 while we set up a self-catering holiday business. Everything else was put on hold until we knew that there would be enough money in the kitty. Not much fun for the boys and to add to the pressures, John was embarking on his Standard Grades at school. By the early summer things had eased financially and recognising how little we had done for the children over the previous months we decided it was their turn for some treats. John wanted a new bike. The one he fancied was beyond our limit so he could only have it if his dad stumped up the last £50. His dad agreed. The bike would be John's.

Friends were staying to give the cottages a trial run and we all shared a meal in the evening. Their children and ours were as high as kites. They hardly ate a thing, which should have struck us as odd but we put it down to excitement about camping overnight on the ridge above the house. We smugly congratulated ourselves how marvellous to live somewhere with so much freedom, where children can safely camp out alone and enjoy innocent pleasures. Before bed we listened for the children — silence. They must be tired out, we fondly thought. Tired out? No, actually. They were a mile away, breaking into the local primary school, led by the heroic John.

In the morning the boys had returned, grubby and exhausted, to their own beds. We knew nothing of the previous night's activities until the police came to call and all was revealed. They had stolen money and items of stationery, eaten food from the kitchen and taken a knife. John had commandeered most of the booty and stashed it in his sleeping bag. To add insult to injury he had scrawled obscenities all over the schoolchildren's climbing frame. I was deeply upset and extremely angry that he should have done such a thing in our own small and supportive community, in the school that he and his brother had attended. I felt well and truly kicked in the teeth. Other people's kids behave like that, not mine.

We recovered what was left of the money from John and returned it and the other items to the school. Cigarettes he had bought were returned to the shop. He seemed to be going for the full range of vices in one fell swoop. We cancelled the new bike as a punishment, but it seemed to have little effect on John's behaviour. He was sullen, resentful and aggrieved by our action. It never seemed to occur to him that any of it was his fault. He thought our sole purpose in life was to give him a bad time and from then on, John and I did little more than tolerate each other.

With a year to go before his exams, John's father and new girlfriend started to suggest that John should move to live with them, attending a local sixth-form college to do his A levels. Theatre Studies and Film Studies weren't available at his school and I could appreciate the limitations of life for a teenager in a remote Scottish village. But, though John and I were hardly on the best of terms, I still didn't want him to go. His father's enthusiasm seemed to be more about impressing the new girlfriend with his caring-parent credentials than concern for John's education – and previous girlfriends hadn't lasted the length of an A-level course. Where would that leave John?

No matter how difficult life with John had become, letting go seemed harder. It was difficult not to feel betrayed by his desire to live with the father who had done so little for him over the years and who had no idea what he would be taking on. As far as he and his partner were concerned, John was a mature young man who would fit into their household well. After all, they told me, he would be living with people who were teaching the very subjects he would be studying. I tried to explain the problems, but it was very clear that they thought if anyone had a problem it was me. In the end I agreed that he could apply for a place – with the proviso that he had to settle down and put some hitherto non-existent effort into his schoolwork to prove that he was mature enough to handle college. Yes, of course he would. Promises, promises – they slipped so easily off his tongue.

But, with his escape route secured, John lost all interest in making the most of his life with us. He was well and truly focused on the fool's gold of life with his father. Despite reminders from me that his move to college depended on a demonstration of maturity and honesty, he continued to tell lies and steal from us. He knew and I knew that his departure was assured so long as he managed to pass 5 Standard Grades and he was smart enough to manage that with the minimum of effort.

One day John asked for money to get his hair cut. I had no change so gave him a £10 note. He arrived home and made a fairly large production of giving me the £5 change. Alarm bells rang somewhere in the back of my head. When he turned to leave the kitchen I got a good view of the 'haircut'. His hair had certainly been cut, but not by any hairdresser. It took a while and numerous implausible stories, but eventually he admitted that a mate had cut it because the money had been stolen from his pocket in the morning. No, he hadn't reported the theft because he didn't think it was all that important. It was obvious to me that no haircut was ever intended. I was angry, very angry. To be lied to again and treated like a complete idiot made me furious. I shouted till my throat hurt. I trashed his bedroom, tipping out drawers, emptying bags and overturning mattresses looking for the cigarettes I presumed he'd bought. All way over the top, of course, but I was consumed with rage. I found nothing.

Later that day, John asked to speak to me alone. It was like this; he'd been in the toilets and had noticed a small foil-wrapped package on the floor. He'd picked it up and taken it to the classroom. The teacher had walked in and before he knew it, the police were being called. I knew he was lying. It wasn't hard to work out the truth for myself. He'd spent the 'haircut' money on drugs. All I felt was exhaustion. I reminded John that no further action had been taken on the school break-in because he was a first-time offender. He wouldn't be let off so lightly a second time – possession of drugs was far more serious. He could say goodbye to college.

A few long and unpleasant days later there was a phone call from the police. The drug had been analysed. It was aspirin and bicarbonate. Pretty effective if he'd had a headache with a touch of indigestion. It turned out he'd been pressured into buying the 'drug' by someone he thought was his friend. John had been taken for a mug. Quite a lesson.

His school excluded him for three weeks before his exams as an example to other would-be drug offenders. On his readmittance, he made a promise to me and the school that from then on he would work hard and finish his time at the school in an honourable way. Another worthless promise. Once the exams were over he had no interest in school anymore and started missing classes. A week before the end of term the final letter came. Don't come back to school – you can't be bothered and neither can we. Well, they didn't put it quite like that but we got the general idea.

That was when I finally decided to make life easy on myself and let him have what he wanted right away.

Two days later John and I were on our way to Gretna to meet his father. There was no proper farewell dinner or celebration of his independence and new life. How had we got to this point, I wondered?

His father and girlfriend were already there. She launched into how they would go to his college the next week and get his reading list and how she might do film studies as well. Her insensitivity was breathtaking. I excused myself, managing to contain the tears until I reached the car. John came after me. 'Don't cry, Mum,' he said, 'I'm not going away forever.' Then we hugged and said we loved each other and I told him he could always come back if it didn't work out. Then he moved his bags from the back of my car to hers and that was it – he was gone and effectively it was forever.

I cried all the way to Glasgow. I didn't have a car radio, so there was just me and my head and this great gaping void. I had no idea that losing John would hurt so much. Only days before I had been counting the days till he left, looking forward to the peace his absence would bring. But instead of relief all I could feel was pain and bitterness.

John has been home twice in the last year. None of us enjoyed the visits very much. It's as if he only comes to sneer at the boring country bumpkins now that he's where it's all happening.

And is he happy? His once hardly noticeable stammer has worsened significantly, and his previously unbitten fingernails are now chewed to the quick. He says he's happy. His dad lets him do what he likes, when he likes, and I have to grit my teeth, keep quiet and hope that John will manage to stay out of trouble. It's hard to switch off after sixteen years, but I'm starting to get the hang of it. There isn't really much choice.

One down, two to go. I can hardly wait.

The Puffball Offering

Elisavietta Ritchie

I found the grass,
smashed his ebullience.
My world was smashed.

Two weeks we've sparred like damaged gulls
clawing in corners, tar on our wings,
screeching, or speechless.

One cannot, cannot, live like that.
At last it seems he's put aside
his stormy moods.

The weather also puts up a good front
before November, so
since it's Sunday, we drive to the woods.

Walking alone with his new shepherd pup —
childhood snatched back, consolation, bribe —
he whistles, throws sticks, spooks the sheep,

then discovers a puffball
big as a skull, beige as a bone,
it thumps like a softball.

He bears it home like a baby squirrel.
Roots like hairs clutch dirt.
My knife slides through that porous sphere.

Odd the earth's excrescences
should be so white inside . . .
The lead-coloured worm doesn't faze us.

Slice after slice we fry in hot butter,
eat them only with pepper and salt,
hoping, unspoken, for magical journeys

but relieved that we stay on the earth
beside our first fire of this fall,
and smell mushroom, butter, wood smoke and wet dog.

And we know: this is only a truce,
a swift feast of peace, a perching on earth,
a brief huddle.

Lucy

Lynne Smith

My daughter was born in 1973 when I was twenty-five years old. During the late sixties and early seventies I read feminist literature avidly – absorbing advice on parenting and teaching girls to be independent and liberated. It alerted me to the dangers of early conditioning and sex-role stereotyping. I hoped my son, born the previous year, would grow up to be compassionate and liberal-minded and that my daughter would be a free spirit, unrestricted by expectations traditionally associated with her gender.

Looking back, it is hard to disentangle the complex experiences which have shaped a child's life. Having an older brother undoubtedly influenced Lucy's early choice of friends and activities. Other girls, their pastimes and toys didn't hold much interest for her. She was never happier than when she was building bonfires or fishing in the canal with a group of boys. She was fiercely independent and developed a healthy taste for adventure. At primary school she shone and teachers praised her natural curiosity and winning ways.

At upper school she chose options with a view to studying medicine. Special dispensation was given so that, contrary to school policy, she could study three sciences. She was given a place in the Russian class, a privilege granted to only a few.

Exactly one year later, when she reached fifteen, everything changed. She became moody and sullen. Always an early riser, she now only put in an appearance five minutes before leaving the house for 'school'. On returning from wherever she had spent her time that day, she would disappear up to her attic bedroom, emerging briefly for the evening meal, only to disappear again until the next morning. As usual, in times of domestic stress, meal times were a continual battle-ground, where old and new grievances were aired unrelentingly. Our lives, though inextricably intertwined by the same four walls, took their separate tracks.

Boyfriends meant something different now and she gave a lot of attention to her appearance. Lucy imperceptibly slid out of anything resembling school uniform. The Gothic phase began. She was clothed in black from head to toe with carefully contrived designer scruffiness; her pale, defiant features relieved only by heavily defined black eye sockets. She rarely washed or showered and her clothes never found their way to the washing basket unaided. When she did make a rare change of clothing, the soiled ones were left in heaps around her bedroom. Her bedroom itself echoed her frame of mind; soft toys and books disappeared and in their place cassettes. ash-trays and beer cans proliferated.

Homework stopped. It became difficult to control where she went, what time she went out and what time she came in. Girlfriends loomed large and she was fiercely loyal to them. Any enquiries about friends, school, where she had been, where she was going, what she had been doing, met with a wall of silent hostility. She never initiated a conversation and thinly disguised bitterness and resentment seethed continuously beneath the surface. Moodiness and unpredictability replaced her good-natured at-one-ness with the world.

Money started to disappear. So did alcohol. I began to be very worried. Then, on one occasion, a large number of bottles of wine and spirits disappeared. I felt that we couldn't ignore Lucy's behaviour, hoping it was due to the usual adolescent grumpiness and waiting for it to go away. This was clearly very serious. We decided to investigate. We questioned Lucy but she strongly denied any knowledge of the theft. Suspecting that she was lying, we started to ask her friends if they knew anything. Eventually a group of friends confessed that she had stolen a large quantity of alcohol to share with them.

We went to speak to Lucy about this, but she refused to say one word. Then shortly afterwards, to our horror, she made a suicide attempt. Although this was absolutely terrifying, at least this meant that my growing fears for Lucy were not unfounded. Something was badly wrong. At last this was being seen and acknowledged by the outside world. Lucy was hospitalised and assigned a psychiatrist. But, deceived by her apparent conformity, the psychiatrist had her quickly discharged.

I hoped and prayed that Lucy was as well as the authorities seemed to think but at the start of the crucial GCSE examinations, she ran away from home. We tried to contact her, but she wouldn't meet with, or speak to, us. I kept in touch with her whereabouts through talking to friends whose children heard news of her. She was leading a semi-vagrant existence. Many of her friends were at the age when their parents left their offspring whilst they went on holiday. These staggered absences meant that a succession of temporary accommodation was made available (which the parents were blissfully unaware of). We were to learn later that she also 'squatted' in the once-resplendent residences of the wool barons of the town, now left vacant and rotting.

We were bewildered, frightened, powerless. We had no way of making contact with her. Social services and other agencies could offer no help because, from the age of sixteen, young people can live where they like and, within the law, do what they like. I found this very hard to accept but there was no way that I could intervene and help her to redirect her life.

A year after rejecting school because it was 'boring' she was to be found working on an industrial sewing machine in a firm which paid abysmally low wages. She later left this to become a care assistant in an old people's home. A senior assistant confided in me that she was a 'born nurse'. We were successful at making some contact with her and encouraged her to think about entering at the local college of nursing. By the time she had passed the entrance examination, she was pregnant. The father of the child is violent, in and out of gaol, and a drug addict.

Theories constantly proliferate attempting to explain why so many teenage girls fail miserably to achieve their potential and become disaffected with home and school. Peer-group pressure is a close candidate for first place. It is argued that girls quickly learn that academic achievement can make them unpopular with boys who feel threatened and don't want to be overshadowed. But why do some girls succumb to these pressures while others remain immune? Teenagers often rebel when overzealous parents try to dictate their lives. Yet often families with a very high degree of conformity and discipline produce girls who do realise their full potential.

Lucy is nineteen. Her current absorption in domesticity forms a sharp contrast to the preoccupations and aspirations of her old classmates, many of whom are beginning their university careers. Sometimes I look at all the aspirations I had for her as a young woman growing up with all the benefits established by feminism and the women's liberation movement. Then I remind myself that it is her life, and that this is only the beginning of it.

Hazel

Jean Buffong

It was a normal winter's evening. Everyone in the family was in. Eight-year-old Marcia was reading her latest comic while ten-year-old Gary and his father fought over which television programme to watch. I had just gone upstairs when the doorbell rang. Thinking it was a salesman taking advantage of the bad weather, hoping to find most people indoors, I ignored it. I had started sorting out school clothes for the next day when it rang again. This time it sounded as if someone was calling my name. No one else seemed to have heard it. I went to the door and opened it.

There, on the doorstep, half-frozen and clasping a small holdall tightly in her hand, was my brother's thirteen-year-old daughter, Hazel.

'Good evening . . . aunty,' she greeted me through chattering teeth. For a moment, I thought I was dreaming. I stared at the child.

'Good evening,' she repeated.

'Oh, sorry luv, sorry, good evening. Come in come in.' I

pulled her inside, continuing to stare at her in amazement. What on earth was she doing here, all alone, on this cold miserable evening? I wondered. How had she got from Sheffield to London? Surely her parents would never allow her to travel by herself?

It was about two years since I had last seen my niece. She had been a cheeky, full-of-herself little madam, then, full of life. She was into everything: school drama group, church choir, community group. Everything. And she excelled at school. What *could* have happened? Her father, Geoff, regularly phoned me with the family gossip, and asked my advice about family matters. As the only two in the family living in England we supported each other as much as possible. But I hadn't had a hint of this.

I looked at the child standing in front me. The once-plump blackcherry-mischievous cheeky face was now sullen and ashen. The bright demanding eyes were veiled. Clearly, the young person before me was carrying the world's burden on her back.

As I was standing there, totally bewildered, my husband Jack joined me in the hallway. 'Hello, Hazel!' he said in astonishment. Then he looked at me, read the trouble in my eyes, and went back to the television.

'Hazel, what you doing in London?' I finally asked. 'Where is your father?'

I stretched my hand to touch her, but she shrank away.

Eyes bowed to her toes she whispered, 'Can I stay here for a few days?'

My thoughts were running haywire. What was this child doing in London, looking so miserable and rejected?

I took her coat and hung it on the peg. 'Would you like a hot drink? Tea or drinking chocolate?'

Still clasping her case tightly in her hand she followed me into the kitchen.

'Have you eaten?' I asked. She shook her head. Then the tears started.

'Never mind . . . never mind. It will be all right.' I hugged her, but her shoulders stiffened. Through the thin jumper she wore I could feel her bones. 'Never mind, it will be all right,' I repeated.

I made her a cup of drinking chocolate and a sandwich, and stood watching her begin to eat. Almost immediately, the phone rang.

A very distraught Geoff was shouting into the phone, almost before I had lifted the handset. 'It's Hazel. We don't know what happen to her,' he was saying, 'O God, I don't know what happen to the child . . . I don't know what happen to her. She gone . . . she missing . . . she . . .'

'Geoff, Geoff,' I broke in. 'Geoff, calm down, calm down. Calm down, *please.*'

'You don't understand! Hazel is missing! She gone since yesterday.'

'Yesterday! What do you mean yesterday? Where did she sleep last night?'

'I, I mean we don't know. We thought she was with Juliet – that's Silvie's daughter. She had asked the mother for her to spend a couple of days with the girl, they usually spend time with each other. It's when Juliet phoned for her we find out Hazel missing. Juliet say she hadn't seen Hazel since Monday and then we find that she took a case with some clothes and I missing some money from my wallet. Her mother gone down to the police station since morning.'

'She is here,' I said as calmly as possible. 'She is here with me.'

'What you mean, she is with you! Sis, you not listening to me; Hazel my daughter, your niece, is missing!'

'I heard you. I was going to phone you but you beat me to it. Hazel is here in London. A few minutes ago there was a knock on the door and there she was. Right now she is having something to eat.'

'You say that Hazel is in London? How did she get there? Is she all right? I don't believe it!'

'She is right here. Geoff, what's going on?'

'Sis, I don't know, to be honest I don't know. The child change so much I just don't know. Thank God she is sensible enough to come to you. Thank you, Sis, thanks. I'll be down tomorrow. We'll talk . . . we'll talk. I don't have to ask you to take care of her; I know she is safe. Thanks, Sis.' Geoff seemed to have aged during the few minutes' conversation. 'Thanks, Sis,' he repeated. 'I'll see you tomorrow. You sure she all right?'

'As far as I can see, but I think she is a bit tired. And you sound drained. Go and get Ruth out of the police station. See you tomorrow.'

I put the family in the picture as much as possible. I told them I didn't know what was going on, but that Hazel would be staying in the spare room for now.

I went back to the kitchen. Hazel sat with the cup in her hand staring into space. The sandwich had not been touched since I left the room.

'Can I stay . . . please?' she pleaded.

'That was your dad on the phone. He is very worried.'

'But can I stay? Please?' she repeated. Her voice was trembling.

'Of course you can stay. You're in London, where else would you stay?' But my mind was on other things. She had left home yesterday. Where had she been?

'What Daddy say?' she asked quietly. 'What he say?'

'He said you left home since yesterday morning. Apparently your mother gone to the police.' For a moment, her frightened face became defiant. Then the tears started again.

'All right, all right. Never mind.' I hugged her, and this time she buried her head deep within my arms and sobbed and sobbed.

'They . . . don't . . . like . . . me. Nobody like me. Daddy always shouting at me,' she stammered. 'And . . . and . . . and . . .'

'Never mind, never mind. Tell me about it tomorrow. Right now you could do with some sleep.' She was obviously too upset for questions. A good night's sleep would be the best policy if I wanted any answers.

After quick, formal greetings to the family Hazel settled down in the spare room. All the problems facing parents with teenagers surfaced in my mind. Could Hazel be pregnant? She was only thirteen but it wasn't impossible. Was it a teenage love problem? Was she mixed up with drugs? In some kind of trouble at school? My brain was going round and round, up and down like a ping pong ball.

After the children went to bed, Jack and I spent many hours talking about possible problems. Only one thing was certain. Now that the girl was here with us it had become our problem, too.

Before going to bed I looked in on Hazel. It looked as if she had fallen asleep the moment her head touched the pillow. She looked like an innocent baby, peacefully sleeping with her thumb in her mouth for comfort.

Next morning I braced myself for whatever revelations might lay ahead. I called in sick at work and went to see if Hazel was ready for some breakfast. I knocked on her bedroom door but there was no answer. Assuming she was still asleep, I concentrated on getting Marcia and Gary off to school. Once Jack left for work I knocked again. Again there was no answer.

I walked into the room and was alarmed to see the bed made and the room empty. My heart missed a beat. When did she leave the house? Where did she go? Why did she leave? Then I heard the sniffling coming from behind the wardrobe. I found her there, huddled like a cast-off bundle.

'Hazel, what's the matter? Come on love, don't hide,' I coaxed her. 'Come out. Nobody will hurt you. You know Aunty won't let anybody hurt you.' I spent about half-an-hour gently talking to her. Trying to get her to talk to me. Tell me something; anything. I sat on her bed and talked to her, talked and talked. Eventually she came out.

'Don't send me back, please. Don't let Daddy take me back,' she whispered. 'Please let me stay.'

I hugged her. 'Don't worry, love,' I said, 'don't worry. Whatever it is we'll sort it out.'

Geoff and Ruth arrived just after eleven. I was hoping that they could resolve my confusion, but they had little more information than me. They repeated that her personality seemed to have changed, but couldn't say why or when it began. Now she only spoke when she felt like it and that was not very often, even with her friends at school. From the bright outgoing child I'd known, she had become almost a young recluse. She was withdrawn and sullen. She would fake illnesses so that she wouldn't have to go to school, and now her school results were poor. Her parents had been discussing finding some help, wondering if they could find a counsellor, and thought she might have been alarmed by that. But why she should go to such lengths as running away, no one could understand.

Her parents spent three days in London. They tried to talk to Hazel, but all she would say is she refused to go home, and that she'd run away again if they made her. After much debate and discussion Jack and I agreed to have her to stay with us for the time being.

That was over five years ago. Five years of looking after Hazel's needs. Nurturing, counselling and loving her; making her feel that she belongs – that she is safe with us.

It hasn't been easy. There are times when Hazel won't speak, won't answer my questions, won't ask any. We never knew what to expect from school. Often teachers would call at their wits' end because Hazel wouldn't participate in lessons. Some days she could be very cheerful. At those times she would be loving and caring, and very protective of Marcia. But most of the time she was strange and morose. One day, when she came home from school, her head resembled a patchwork shaggy stripped mop. Hazel had decided that her lovely thick black hair needed cutting, and had taken to it with blunt scissors and a knife. Before I could ask why she informed me that it was her hair and she could do what she liked with it.

Sometimes she would be silent for days on end. Sometimes she could be very aggressive, shouting that I didn't care about her, I wasn't doing anything to help, I was just like all the rest.

Jack lost patience when she behaved like that. 'Why don't you send the girl back to her parents?' he would shout. 'Why are we going through all these problems with her? She's not our child! You say it's just a phase she going through. But she been going through it for years!'

But I knew that Hazel needed the sort of help that her family, though caring and loving, could not give her alone. They were too close and the effort to understand and deal with her problems was too painful for them all. Hazel had to learn to love herself again. And she needed space from her family to find that out.

I discovered among other things that she'd had no preparation for her periods starting, and I had to spend months persuading her that periods were natural. I had a strong sense that she hated her growing body and had to try and make her see herself as a beautiful young woman.

Like most teenagers, Hazel was forever on a diet. I tried to convince her that she was not remotely 'fat', but soon I realised that there was something she was more afraid of than that. All I could do was talk and talk to her, guessing at the source of her troubles and trying to reassure her as much as I could. Sometimes she would fly into furies — once she assaulted me — and sometimes she would weep and sob. But with each outburst I felt she was letting pain out, and allowing herself to heal. I never chastised her, never told her off. But I held her through her tears and never told anyone what had happened.

I believe that made all the difference. Slowly, gradually Hazel transformed from a frightened, bewildered, aggressive young changeling into a beautiful young woman who had learnt to love herself. It has not been easy nurturing Hazel through her painful teenage years, but as I watch her now as she moves about, her back straight, her head upright, full of confidence, I think of Yabba the African Queen.

The battle is not over yet. As long as life goes on a battle is being fought, but we are living, living and winning.

Notes for Teenagers for when Mum's Away

Carolyn Giles

1. Preparing your clothes for the washing machine

(a) running colours

If you put dark or brightly coloured things in with white or light ones, the white ones won't be. Embarrassingly pink shorts, lemon school shirts and artistically blotchy grey T-shirts are recent examples – and yes, the gunmetal grey bra is an exclusive colour, Jay, but now shows through lots of your tops.

Keep whites with whites and dark things with dark and you stand a better chance.

But see also (b) emptying pockets, etc.

(b) emptying pockets, etc.

You may have noticed that I swear whenever I hear clanking sounds coming from the washing machine and then either have to stop it and open the door – which involves flooding water all over the kitchen – or bring in the engineer, which is a very EXPENSIVE way of cleaning your 5p coins, keys, lead shot, or chunk of copper pipe.

Please clear out pockets COMPLETELY before putting your clothes in the washing basket.

This will also avoid blotches on pockets (and other washing) from pens, coloured tissues and £20 notes – an EXPENSIVE way of tie-dying. As you have discovered, £20 notes rarely iron well, either.

Similarly, taking your pants out of your trousers, Lee, will avoid those embarrassing, if novel, dye lines. It might be all right for Superman in flight, but less appropriate for us earth-bound mortals who have to walk the High Street.

(c) shrinking

As you have found out, some materials don't like being washed at 90°. Dad was not amused when he had to send his favourite jumper to the toddlers' group. Nor was it diplomatic to suggest that his bobble hat would make a good tea cozy now – the holes appeared in the wrong place for the spout for a start. Though you had a point when you said, 'Maybe he should have done his own washing.'

If you look at the LABEL it should tell you what temperature to set the machine at – 30°, 40°, 50°, 60° or 90° – and our machine has a dial with the 30°, 40° etc. on it. Turn the pointer to the right one – CLOCKWISE please, or as you discovered, the ENGINEER has to call again. The chart on the pinboard on the kitchen wall (top left-hand side) will give you more details for the other dials.

(d) drying

Hanging washing out is so it can get dry air blown round it so it can DRY.

If you bunch 5 socks into 1 peg, it can't.

Leaving it out in the rain doesn't help either.

Pegging things by the seams can help avoid those nasty

stretch and pull marks you complain about so much – so you won't have to spend so much effort ironing things.

I know the tumble drier avoids many of these problems, but it is EXPENSIVE, so should only be used if you really cannot get things dry in time by hanging out. Oh yes, and a reminder – your having forgotten to wash something in plenty of time is NOT a sufficient emergency to run the washing machine and tumbler just for one thing.

(e) ironing

Again the LABEL on the garment will show you the setting, and the new iron we had to buy recently is nice and modern so it has a dial on it with those symbols too. Turn the dial so the symbol is by the dot.

If you're not sure, go for the coolest.

Before we had that accident, Lee, you probably hadn't thought about it being important WHERE you do the ironing. I'm sure you won't forget, but just a reminder – it is not a good idea to have the ironing board up round a blind corner in the middle of the passage that people and animals often dash along.

And another reminder, wandering off to watch that crucial bit of the tennis (or was it football?) was what caused the hole in the shirt – and the ironing board. DON'T leave a hot iron on clothes EVER. And put it somewhere to cool down where it won't get knocked by people or animals or hurt them.

2. Cleaning and tidying up

(a) washing you

The purpose of washing your hands is to get them clean – and that does not mean wiping the dirt off on the towel. Having washed them is not enough. Nor 'I washed them this morning.'

Are they CLEAN? NOW? Same for the rest of you.

(b) tidying

Basically you have to tidy up so things don't get trodden on and broken, or hurt people who tread on them. Also so things don't get lost.

When you drop something, pick it up, NOW. Picking it up and nearly putting it safely on the surface doesn't count –it's still on the floor.

Similarly, if you are throwing something away, put it *in* the bin, not just near it.

And when you've finished using something, put it away – BACK WHERE IT CAME FROM. I know sometimes you don't understand why we keep some things on the shelves, others in cupboards, the shed, the attic or garage. But I do . . .

(c) hoovering

The Hoover is not a machine to clear up bits you can't be bothered to pick up – only dust. It suffers from similar problems to the washing machine when asked to eat 'foreign bodies'. And is similarly EXPENSIVE when it eats coins and £10 notes. £1.45p last time I cleaned your bedroom, Jay. And NO, Lee, the asthma you had 10 years ago is NOT a good enough excuse for not fishing money out of the Hoover bag when you hear it go in. Nor is not hearing it because you had your Walkman going at the time.

(d) washing up

Like washing you and tidying really – clean (NO grease or bits), dry and away by the time I'm back please.

3. Petcare

(a) fish

When you can't see the fish because the water is so green, it needs new water – of the same temperature or it will get a nasty shock.

It helps if you open the curtains so you can see if you can see the fish.

(b) cats

Some cats have been known to be able to 'perform' on human loos when desperate – ours, to date, can't. Nor can the

(c) dog

They all need letting out regularly. Despite how fascinating the video is, if they scratch at the door, it means NOW.

They also need feeding. You know the food, the amount and the times. So if you get it wrong, be prepared to be LOOKED AT, NIBBLED or worse, depending on your level of forgetfulness.

4. Food?

(a) what food?

Anything which is in the cupboards, fridge or freezer. Now is the time to eat whatever you fancy, so you don't have to moan about what I cook. There's plenty there.

NB The bottles are on the cupboard, not in it, so are out of bounds. And don't try the re-filling the bottles up with water or the cold tea trick again – nor anything else.

(b) how to cook it

The frozen stuff has instructions on it for defrosting and cooking – follow them.

The cookbooks are on the shelf in the kitchen on the right-hand side of the cooker.

So cook any way you choose, really. Keep an eye on it ALL the time and don't use the smoke alarm as a 'done' indicator.

One exception: NO BARBECUES

5. Emergencies

Doctor, dentist, vet and Grandma are all listed in our house phone book, which is the stripey one in the top drawer of the desk, in the lounge, next to the window.

You probably don't need reminding, but anyway: 999 for Police, Fire and Ambulance if it's a real emergency. And yes, the barbecue was; no, the cat being sick wasn't.

Yellow Pages can be very useful e.g. for broken windows. And out of your pocket after your party, not my credit card – yes, I will notice; I do check the bill.

And lastly, lastly, PLEASE could you carry on doing these bits and pieces when I'm back?

Have a good time.
Love
Mum
XX

Nights in the Graveyard

Rosalind Brackenbury

The cop stood in the hall looking puzzled. I'd just given him a description of my missing son.

'I don't know how you can lose someone like that,' he said. He had a small notebook but hadn't yet written anything down. 'Could you tell me that again?'

'He's fifteen, he's in a wheelchair, he's got tattoos on his arms, he's wearing a leather jacket and a homburg hat.'

'Jings,' said the cop. He wrote. It took him some time, with pauses in between words. He was a tall, ginger-haired Edinburgh man with pink hands. There was another one there too, looking all around him as if looking for something to suspect. I suppose it was a habit, looking for clues. But it didn't do anything to calm me down.

'Well, are you going to look for him, or what?'

'We don't go looking for someone till they've been missing twenty-four hours,' the ginger one said. 'Now, how did you spell your name? In a wheelchair, you said? Could you describe the wheelchair? Was it a normal one?'

'Normal? Well, NHS, sort of battered-looking, with stickers. Heavy metal stickers.'

'Heavy metal.'

'The music.'

'Oh, aye. Heavy metal.' He pronounced it with elongated Es, Edinburgh style. He wrote it down.

'You mean you won't do anything tonight?'

'No, madam. If we went off looking for everybody — I mean, a lot of mothers do get worried. Teenagers go off a lot. We'd be out all night.'

'But a person could be dead, in twenty-four hours.' I had to voice my worst thought to somebody.

'Aye, but usually they're not. You'll call us if he comes back in?'

It was then that you rang the doorbell. I knew it was you, because you kept your thumb on it and because that long urgent peremptory ring was the way you announced yourself home. I'm back, come at once, I'm out of money, or I need a pee. I opened the front door. Yes, you in your battered wheelchair, your hat on sideways, you jumping with impatience to get to the toilet, and a taxi out there on the kerb with a tired man waiting to be paid. Love and fury. Relief and resentment. All at once, as usual. I heave you in through the door and propel you towards the bathroom. The two cops are still in the hall, getting in the way. I want to say to them, just fuck off out of here, will you. It's two in the morning and the cold night air's rushing into my already chilly house. It's at times like these that I long for there to be someone else, someone calm, sane and helpful, who knows what to do; perhaps a calm, sane version of myself who has not yet appeared. I go down the steps and give the taxi man a fiver because he's dragged you out of a bar somewhere and pulled you up the steps to the front door, every one of those stone steps a backbreaker that these posh old Edinburgh houses couldn't do without. You're in the toilet a long time, cursing.

The cops have that crackle of static about them, they're wired up to somewhere else, their little machines come on and nag at them. The cab man smiles a bit and thanks me and gets back into his cab. I'm always either thanking people too much or apologising to them and tipping them too much, these days. It's a way of trying to make all this work.

When you come rolling out at last, zipping your fly with one hand and that hat still jaunty on your head, you say, 'Hey, Mum, what you got the fuzz here for? Something gone wrong?'

Then they start on you. Two of them at once, grown men with their nagging accents and the voices still coming on from their chests where they wear their radios. They go on about irresponsibility and getting people out in the middle of the night. Their voices lean on you, they shout down their threats, two men in black uniforms getting at one tired boy who can't even stand up to answer back. Not that you usually do without answering back, but this time you are silenced. After a minute, I can't stand it. I open the front door and yell, 'Go! Go! We don't need you here!' I don't remember what they say, I'm too angry. All my anger's suddenly for them, because I can't be angry at you any more, because you're back.

'Good for you, Mum,' you say, lighting up a cigarette in the hallway.

'Another time I'll know not to call the police, they don't even start looking for someone till they've been missing twenty-four hours, and they could be dead in a ditch by then.' Dead in a ditch seems to be something I have been needing to say for some time. 'Now, where the hell have you been?'

'What's the matter, Mum? Cool it, I was only in a bar. I met up with some great Irish people. We were down in Leith. I would have phoned you only I couldn't reach the phone, it was by the toilets and they were down a whole load of steps.'

'But it's after two! The pubs closed hours ago.' Both of us have forgotten that you're not supposed to be in a pub at all.

'Well, they took me home with them. We were having great

crack. They called me a cab. I would've stayed, only I thought you'd be worried.'

'You thought I'd be worried? You could have started thinking that four hours ago. Give me a cigarette, will you?'

'What's the hassle, Mum? You don't have to worry about me. I'm a survivor. Don't you know that by now? You worried about me ending up in a wheelchair, or something?'

I don't say that I've been through all the fears in the book, the ones every mother of teenagers knows, the abductions, the rape, the beating-up, the murder. It's like inside all of us at times like this, all there is, is a memory of war. The war of the world against young defenceless people, our children. The one that sends news from its front lines every single day. In these memories there's nobody being good, friendly or decent, nobody calling cabs to get you home. There's just mindless violence, senseless threat. At 2 a.m. it's pretty damn hard to keep these memories, these dire scenarios, out.

I don't know — do you? — how many times this scene was repeated in our life together at that time, the one in which our roles are divorced mother and rebellious teenage son? It seemed to go on for years. There was the night you didn't come back at all, when I realised that there was nothing I could do about it, so I might as well sleep. There was the time you rang the doorbell at five and came back in, dew-soaked, filthy and smelling of rum, saying you'd spent the night in the graveyard. There was the day I flew in from a conference in America and heard that you and a drunken friend had taken my uninsured car and driven it into a wall. You were both at the police station, shaken but unharmed. The friend who'd been looking after you had not noticed that you had not been to school all that week. There was the drinking and the smoking and the flirtation with drugs. 'Don't worry, at least I can't get legless,' was one of your favourite jokes. There were the Houdini-like disappearances: how the hell can someone in a wheelchair get out of a house that fast? There was the smell of sweat, marijuana and aftershave all one summer, that meant that your friends were round, camped in your bedroom, the shutters closed. There was food disappearing and money disappearing. There was your teacher endlessly on the phone talking about truanting, smoking, answering back, and who set fire to the classroom.

All this is pretty familiar stuff to the parents of adolescents, and at the time, when it seemed endless and I endlessly tired, it was easy not to notice anything else. Now I see it as the growing-up of a young disabled man in Britain in the glitzy eighties. What you were doing was yelling at me, about what it was really like. You pushed and shoved and fought me from complaining mother to radical accomplice. I hated it, but gradually understood that I had to stand by you, while letting you go. You were fighting for your freedom, your self-respect, your place in the world, all the things which society said you could not have. And what you demanded of me was what every young person needs, an ally, someone who will stick by you no matter what. The process dragged out all my fears, my prejudices, my assumptions, into the light of day; all my education, class-conditioning and anxiety about the world, all the élitism and 'niceness' in which I'd been brought up. You taught me what it means to be disabled in a society which turns so many blind eyes and flaunts such hypocrisy. You showed me which side of the tracks to be on, the one you're on for good. I'm not going back.

'I don't know how you can lose someone like that,' the cop said. Well, you can't. The images are there with you for life. You, too, live in a world of steps, narrow doorways, methods of transport you can't get on, films you can't see, people you can't visit, jobs you can't get, bathrooms you can't use. You start off like everyone else, expecting the perfect baby with everything working, a little extension of yourself and your family. With a child with disabilities, whoever they are, they are not that. So you have to start learning, shifting, moving through the pain, start thinking clearly, start seeing what's what. You get a crash course in oppression. You learn what unreliable guides to reality expectations are. And you find out that your best ally and informant is your child. Your child knows the score better than you do and is a better bullshit detector by far. You'd better listen, you'd better learn, and you'd better get tough.

I look back now on your teenage years and think, that was some roller-coaster; but long-term, I don't think it did either of us any harm. I didn't ever feel that your rage and violence was directed at me. It wasn't personal. It had a wider target, I just happened to be in the way. It was like living with a loving terrorist, a contradiction which can and does exist.

I remember a note you wrote me after one of those nights when I'd raged at you and said I couldn't stand it any more. You pushed it under my bedroom door, and I found it in the morning. Its gist was this:

> Dear Mum, if you feel angry with me kindly remember that these are your feelings and nothing repeat nothing to do with me. It's just that you had a different upbringing. So don't dump it all on me again. Or else. Your loving son.

You were right, of course, and you were asking me to let go. At the same time society was insisting on the opposite, that you turn up at school, clean up your act, do your homework, do as you were told. It's classic. If I didn't have such vivid memories of similar scenes myself – black sweaters, black eye make-up, lectures to my parents on Free Love and Marxism, and the whole smoking-drinking-sex-parties debate – maybe I'd have been a harder nut to crack. But for us who grew up in the fifties and sixties, it isn't so hard to hear from our sons and daughters that society is oppressive and many of its tenets: school, work, toeing the line, fraudulent. If you do this, you'll get that. We saw through the lie decades ago. We were never going to say the things our parents said.

It's just if you get scared and isolated enough that you get hooked. That's what happens to parents, especially divorced parents and especially the parents of disabled children. So I was lucky in my friends and neighbours – friends who held me while I cried out my despair, friends who reminded me that I was a good mother, friends who involved themselves with my son, the friend who drove around the bars of Leith at midnight looking for him, the friend who called me in the morning to ask how things were. My daughter, who had to live through many of these scenes too, while going through her own difficulties. All this makes the crucial difference, when you feel so much on your own.

There's one more scene. We're on our way to the railway station, friends are driving us there, your luggage is packed, and you're leaving. You're on your way. I got the message, it's weaning time.

We had a big fight the day before, one which wrecked a lot of things in the kitchen and had you grabbing a kitchen knife to wave at me. Luckily you'd also taught me some good grips for making people let go of things. I knew it was our last fight. I knew that I would not give way. You were leaving, I had decided, you were going to college in the south of England, and you were going to live with your father. Time to be with the men. I was letting go.

You still weren't speaking to me from the back of that car, as our neighbour drove us to the station. The chips were down, though, and I was at last acting on what you'd been telling me with increasing urgency and what I knew made sense. Time to go.

In the train you turned suddenly light-hearted. You slid on to the seat and looked out of the window and said to me something I think I'll never forget. 'You know what, Mum?'

'No, what?'

'I think you're giving me a kick up the backside at exactly the right moment.'

We laughed and laughed, both close to tears. Then I said goodbye.

Here are two poems that I wrote at about this time. They show me now where some of the conflict lay: they hint at my own, or a woman's, inability to claim the same freedoms as a man. Staying out late, feeling impervious, calling up to say we're not coming home. There's a basic selfishness in adolescent males that takes your breath away. We've been trained to shake in our beds beneath covers and bide our time. So, in the poems, the 'boy in her' 'shouting for recognition, demands to be heard' strikes me, these years later, as a part of myself I'd never admitted or listened to. I spent several years in my forties, after this, coming home late, not coming home at all, running 'scared and daring/ into trouble around the corner'; in short, behaving rather like my young son, only with him out of the way. He'd shown me something I needed to do, and that was probably why it all felt so uncomfortable. 'The woman . . . cannot embrace herself entirely/ will wait no more.' So the time, and his behaviour and then the poem, taught me. Mothers are supposed to be such goody-goodies. Perhaps our 'wild teenagers', as Kathleen Raine described my children once, are there to show us how insufferable we ourselves have become.

The Boy I.

The boy I never was,
streetwise, swaggering,
wears black leather;

the woman you wanted
cannot embrace herself entirely,
will wait no more;

the boy is out there
whistling in the sharp wind;

his heart fills his chest
clean as a wound clock
boxed against complaint;

there is no guessing
what he will become.

The Boy II.

the boy is out all night
in the black wicked weather,

calls from a phone box briefly,
in a bar noisy with coins falling,

shacks up with wild men across town,
sings in a sharp new year,

grips life in hands already callused,
will not listen;

runs scared and daring
into trouble around the corner,

comes in with the wet late dawn;

the woman is in her bed
wakeful, shaking beneath covers,

still prey to the white moon,
she bides her time;

the boy in her rises
shouting for recognition

demands to be heard.

When Words Hurt

Marie Guise Williams

It cannot be denied that the quickest way to expand a child's vocabulary is to get a divorce. And I don't mean good words, for when suddenly the floodgates of verbal abuse burst open between two estranged partners, words you wouldn't have used yourself under different circumstances forge themselves into the path of your child. In this case, my nine year-old-child, Jason.

I, the custodial parent, the one left to clean up the mess, am the one to explain the meaning of these words; these insults and the hefty pieces of divorce law jargon. Fail, and I risk my long term credibility as a source of truthfulness and honesty in his life. As a black woman raising this boy in a tough enough world, the prospect of this disturbs me.

But it isn't easy.

For one thing he looks like his father, that man I have come to despise so much; at nine years old he already imitates the streetwise strut. I see him developing the womanising smile too, witness the growing chauvinism and template for my role in domestic life edging in.

'Where's my dinner, Mom?' he demands, when he swans home late from school to a dormant kitchen. In the morning he yells, 'You should have washed my PE kit,' when he's kept the damned thing hidden beneath his bed all week. He makes these complaints in exactly the same tone as his old man and lately, when he comes back from weekends there, repeats all the horrible things he hears him say. He practises them behind closed doors with his mate Patrick — swear words in Jamaican patois, strong enough and rough enough to make fresh cream curdle.

'Jason!' I scream. 'Do you know what that word means?'

Then when I realise the trap I set myself with such questions, I try and slink away before he asks me to explain.

Maybe I should have handled it better; chosen more caring words, but I was hurt and confused myself. I told my son that my marriage was over by blurting it out at dinner one night. 'God, I hate your dad,' I began my outburst. 'And I'm sick of lying for him. Listen, Jason . . . he's never coming back home. *Ever.*'

My son looked confused. Bewildered. 'What do you mean? Before, you said you were just "separated".'

I threw a wad of paper onto his empty plate. 'Look, this is what they call a decree absolute.'

My son looked weary under the dual burden of this word and the knowledge that his father might never come home. 'What's a decree absolute?'

But I was in no state to explain at that moment. I'd had a few drinks. Tears were making my eyes smart, alcohol blurring the boundaries between cool camaraderie and poor parenting. I wanted him to like me — *side* with me. So I poured myself some more wine, and stupidly tippled a little into his glass. 'Oh well, at least I was awarded custody of you,' I muttered.

The wine was supposed to level us, transform this into a chat between pals but, pushing his glass away, disgusted, Jason's eyes only widened into circles.

'Custody of me? Decree absolute. What's all this, Mum? What does it all mean?'

'Jason.' I momentarily stopped thinking of myself and considered what was at stake for my son. 'Babes, custody is what parents are granted in order to keep the children after they get "divorced". A decree absolute is the piece of paper which means they are "divorced". Your father and I are now "divorced". You do know what that word means, don't you?'

I could almost have mistaken the expression on his face for laughter. 'Of course I do, Mum. Everyone knows what divorce means! But, what I don't understand is how comes you're doing it to me?'

'We're not doing it to you,' I said. 'I'm no longer married to the arsehole, but you'll still get to see him on the weekends. And Jason . . . you can cry, you know. You want to, don't you?'

Jason looked away stubbornly and let out a loud fart. 'No,' he uttered somewhere into his left shoulder. But I knew that wasn't true.

We got over most of the big word legalities, but now instead, a whole year later, he's become a piggy in the middle.

He hears the bad things his father says about me and those I throw back at his father and the woman he left me for, Barbara. 'Bastard', I have taught him; 'chauvinist pig', 'bitch', and 'slag'. And every time Jason goes to stay with them he comes back and tells me something that annoys me more. A couple of weeks ago he came back wearing the gaudiest green bandanna, a true imitation of his father's bad dress sense. But he won't listen. He thinks his father's the bee's knees.

'Mum, I need some new jeans,' he says, throwing down his weekend bag.

But I'm too busy laughing at him behind my *Observer*. 'Yeah, you need some new *genes*, all right – on your father's side. They're throwback.'

Then when I see his eyebrows begin to curl into a question I say, 'Nothing. Just a little joke. How was the weekend?'

'Fine,' he says, as a matter of routine. (He never tells me anything unless directed by his father.)

'Good,' I say. 'Listen, I can't afford the pants this week. Maybe next. But I can't promise. I'm up to my eyeballs in bills.'

'It's okay. I think Barbara wants to buy them for me. 501 jeans. *Levis*. I've never had 501s before.'

I roll the paper baton-like and wave it angrily at him. 'And you won't be wearing them now, either. Are you out of your mind? Have you been begging that woman for money again?'

'No. Honest, Mum.' He steps back as a precaution.

'You better not have,' I warn. ''Cos if I ever catch you begging I'll throw your backside out onto the streets and you can find out what it's like begging full-time. Do you hear me?'

'I hear you.'

'Your father's dying to hear that I can't look after you properly. And his tart, his bit of strumpet, that *slapper*, I don't want to hear her saying she's had to provide *anything* for you.'

'Okay, okay,' he pleads. 'Just don't start another one of those mad rants about Barbara.'

'Like father, like son,' I poke, and nearly smile, amazed at my son's defence of the woman who wrecked my marriage.

My nine-year-old son nearly smiles back, and just when I pick up the paper to read again, says: 'So, Mum. What exactly is a slapper?'

But that isn't the worst of it. You should hear the things Colwyn says about me. It wasn't so bad when Jason was younger, but now as he approaches double figures he seems to believe them more, repeat them to me with more malice.

Last weekend he comes home. I'm in a good mood, guzzling White rum in the kitchen and vegging out on Caribbean bun. He licks his lips.

'Cut me some.'

'Excuse me, you cheeky sod, but I'm not some kind of slave, you know.'

'I know, I know. But can I have some?'

'It's may I have some.'

'Okay then, *may* I have some.'

'No. You haven't said please.'

By which time he's decided that it might be easier to hack the thing to bits himself. He drags his laden plate over to the table and pulls up the chair opposite me.

'Mom?' he says, with more than a hint of mischief. 'What's peristalsis?'

I nearly choke on my bun. 'What d'you want to know that for?'

'Just because.' He digs one bony finger into his bun, another into me. '*Tell me.*'

'All right! Just stop poking me.' I take another sip from my glass. 'Well . . . if you must know, peristalsis is a medical term . . . for movement of the bowel.'

A nine-year-old has to translate this into his own language.

'What you mean your bum and stuff?' He looks excited and then pauses thoughtfully. 'But what sort of movement of the bowel, Mum?'

'Movement that makes you go to the toilet, silly.'

'What, you mean like eating this bun?'

I clap him playfully on the side of the ear. 'Don't be cheeky. But yes, it's what you're thinking. Peristalsis is the movement of the bowel that makes you dump. *Shit.* I guess you could say it's what makes shit happen.'

My son's eyes twinkle recklessly with this new knowledge. 'Are you sure that's right, Mum?' he asks.

'Of course,' I assure him. 'Why?'

'Because . . .' He walks across the room and only turns in the doorway, 'Dad says that when you open your mouth it's like a wave of peristalsis.'

Then the cheeky little sod's gone.

It's pouring down with rain. The door of the New York cab is flung wide open. Holly Golightly's in the alleyway amongst trash cans and torrential floods looking for Cat. Paul Varjek is about to appear in time for the final kiss. It's the fifth time I've seen *Breakfast at Tiffany's*, and still I cry, lonely and depressed.

It's been a year now, and still I fear loneliness. I have no love life. I'm drinking too much. I am scared of losing my son to his admiration for his father. This is the fucker who sold the family house from under us, then had the audacity to throw the cash down the drain. The rest he uses to buy Jason's affections back in the shape of Power Rangers and Super Nintendoes. Left so badly in debt I cannot rival his material excesses. As a woman I am not sought out as a role model. I love this boy, unreservedly, but though I am the one who feeds him and clothes him, has wiped every dripping orifice in his body at some time in his life, it's the one who deserted camp that is held highest in his esteem, gets to be missed all the time.

So Colwyn and I never meet. Even when exchanging our one offspring. Unable to stand the hypocrisy of this man, I push my son out the door to meet his car outside. Colwyn returns the favour by dropping him back home anonymously, to let himself inside, where I am inevitably waiting.

'You're late,' I say today.

'You're drinking again,' he spits. Something strange happens when he goes to stay with that man. Now aged ten he acts so rude when he comes home. Cocky, even.

He walks across the room now with an air of nonchalance, slightly dragging one leg behind him in an effort to look cool.

He looks stupid. I want to ask him if his leg is broken or something, but I swallow this sarcastic remark.

'Look, boy, I'm fed up of your back chat,' I say instead. 'Cool it. I'm not in the mood.'

'Well. You shouldn't keep drinking.' And then he notices my wet eyes. 'You're crying,' he says in amazement.

'I'm just feeling a little sensitive, that's all.' I say. 'And get your feet off the coffee table.'

My ten-year-old son offers no comfort, only stares.

'Mum,' he says. 'Dad says peristalsis isn't what makes shit happen, but bad attitudes are. He says you have a bad attitude and that's why he divorced you.'

I can't believe my ears. 'So, what, he's blaming *me* for the divorce now? Look, I don't know what he's been saying, but we got divorced because of *his* adultery.'

'Adultery?'

'You heard what I said. And if you want to know what it means, it's simple. Your father was having an affair with Barbara before he divorced me.'

'I don't believe you. That's not what Dad says.'

Having started something he doesn't want to finish Jason goes to get up and leave. But I yank him back onto the couch.

'Look, I know it's hurtful,' I explain. 'And I don't mean it to be. I want the best for you. But imagine how bloody hurt *I* am. I'm the one who's lonely and left on my own in this house, to bring you up. I've got nobody to turn to. I've got no social life. And week after week I have to put up with you dragging *his shit* into this house. How do you think that makes me feel when you repeat the rude things he says?'

My son's voice starts to waver. 'So? You do it too, slag him off all the time.'

'Yes, and you call me a liar, whereas you think the sun shines out of *his* arse.'

'Well, you *are* a liar,' he says.

I wag a spare finger at him, over my glass of wine. 'Don't call me a liar, I'm warning you,' I say. But he doesn't take heed.

'Well, what about me?' he shouts. 'You don't care about me when you're slagging each other off. And anyway, no matter what *lies* you tell about Dad, at least he's not some drunken, *pisshead* —'

And in a flash I slap him; my hand connects with the side of his face. Hard. There's a hand print there, a scarlet silhouette of adult anger emblazoned against his young, brown skin. He staggers up, places his hands on the affected area, stares hard and confused at me for what seems like ages, then makes one really dramatic bolt for the bathroom.

So I'm outside pleading for him to unlock the door.

'You know you're not supposed to lock the door,' I say, 'Open it now and we'll forget you've been so stupid.'

No response.

'Come on. You're ten now – a voice breaking almost as deep as Barry White's – come out and let's talk about this. *Please*.'

No response.

'Jason, I'm sorry. I didn't mean to hit you,' I plead. 'But you shouldn't have said those horrible things to me. Come on out and let's talk. I know you're crying in there.'

I hear a movement, a whimper.

'I'm not crying.'

'Come on out and prove it.'

'No. Leave me alone. And *you* stop saying horrible things.'

And that's the last I hear from him, before he scarpers out the bathroom window to be with his father – the hero.

Five days go by, Colwyn relishing the power, refusing to give Jason back. I go round there to try and change his mind, but am only greeted with promises of solicitors, fresh custody hearings. Pyjamas under coat, I limp home in the rain.

I am lonely. I am miserable. I am unloved. But most of all, my boy is gone.

He says he hates me, and that I'm a drunk. His words tear at me. How must mine have hurt him?

I spend the days inflicting self-torture by sleeping on the couch not bed, munching dry crackers as punishment and drinking red sauvignon as my only form of solace. At night I wander into his room, hug his pillow, or watch late news programmes where men in suits wield other words manufactured to harm people. I phone in work daily, hoping he might miraculously come back before I need a sick note.

On the fifth night at 10 o'clock the door bursts open. A burglar? For a minute I'm frightened – but then the living-room door opens and against the orange glow of the hallway light I see my little man's silhouette. Colwyn's old banger speeds away outside, guilty as a getaway car. Jason drops his rucksack and starts to turn out of the room.

'Jason,' I say. 'Don't go. I need to talk to you.'

He turns, startled. 'Oh.'

'How are you? I thought you weren't coming back,' I say.

He shrugs his shoulders. 'I wasn't going to at first. But Dad doesn't really want me. So I'm back.

'I heard him telling Barbara in the kitchen this evening — weekend visits are long enough. "There's not enough room for two men in the house." "Cramps his style." Anyway, there'll be barely enough room for weekend visits either soon.' He shuffles about the room all hunched and dejected. 'Barbara's gone and got herself preggers.'

I laugh. 'Pregnant not "preggers", don't be vile,' I say. 'And I don't think she did it by herself. Your father's definitely involved in this one.'

My son looks thoughtful, and I catch the outlines of tears in his round, brown eyes.

'Look, Jason, I've really missed you and I want you back here,' I say. 'But you're gonna have to go with the flow of things while I sort out some problems, get my drinking under control and stuff. And you'll have to cool it on the back chat.'

Jason sort of frowns. 'Did you drink while I was away?'

'No.' I shake my head. 'Oh, okay, yes I did and I'm sorry. But what was I supposed to do? I missed you. I was frightened. I thought you might never come home.'

'Well, I have now, and I don't want you to drink anymore. It makes you mad. You just sit around slagging Dad all the time. He says you need help.'

'And he's probably right for once, if only by accident,' I say. 'But Jason . . . let that be the last time you bring "Dad says" into this house. I mean it. If you do that then I'll try hard to get things back to normal.'

Jason finally lets the tears go, one by one down his soft,

pubescent face. 'I miss him. I wish we could be a family again.'

'I know,' I say. 'But it's so good to see you cry at last.'

He makes a dive for his tears with his sleeve. 'I'm not crying.'

'Of course you aren't. Maybe you just need a hug.'

His ten-year-old nose wrinkles in defiance. 'Naah.' He stands there looking all sheepish for a moment, then positively vulnerable.

'Oh, okay,' he says, then comes lumbering over in the semi-darkness, like he's doing me a favour.

I reach out to receive him, hold him tight.

Soon he'll think he's too cool for this, crying in his mother's arms on a Friday night. He'll want to be out playing pool with his mates. He'll be on dates. He will not come to me to seek help with such matters. Where will he go? To his louse of a father? If so, I fear for my little boy.

'I do love you,' I tell him, wiping the last tear from his face.

'Mom!' Jason says, disgustedly.

He wrenches himself free and escapes to bed.

Waiting

Ruth Smith

The surfaces of your room are impeccable, but
I can't rejoice. Instead I watch the slow drift
of splintered motes through sun and regret removing
that clutter of jostling images from your walls. The bed,
lacking your light impress, remains unruffled;
but don't be deceived. Idling away on those shelves,
the tigerish past is penned up; waiting. One day,
for you too, it will crouch. Just be prepared for its spring.

This, after all, was your growing space; home to the
careful accumulations of those fervid years:
barred hawk's feathers; badges; an adder's cast-off skin.
Over here, the paints that splashed your infant rainbows; journals
that started but broke off to say no more; a card,
embossed with tiny bones. Remember! You laid them out to
itemise the owl's carnage. The natural world yielded
to your inquisitive quest and you learnt its ways.

And here you bent to study or, in truth, you
smouldered over schoolbooks. I'll swear you conjugated
curses to the creaking of that hamster's wheel. Learning
crept in and you let it settle, but your true
yearnings went another way. The world suddenly
tilted and you leaned after it. Fresh pleasures stirred.
Whilst studied circumspection was your chosen guise
you often blew your cover with that secret smile.

And then, the adventurous years. You gained a foothold
in the Alps; traversed time zones and never, ever forgot
one ghostly dusk in templed India. Your orbit
grew, but still the threads that bound you drew you back
to base. You stopped and bivouacked here and your souvenirs
found houseroom. Now, when you return to this laden space
I detect already in you, time's first keenings
as memory ferments its sweet and bitter brew.

Within the Fear

Emma Marx

'Devils,' he yells. My teenage son leaps over the front bumper to land feet first on the Nissan's hood. He cocks his wooden gun and points it at his father, then at me. Only the windshield is between him and us. He presses his face flat against the glass, further distorting his angry mouth, and shakes his fist at us. This son is dangerous.

'It's okay,' his father says to me as he grips my hand. 'The police are on their way. The doors are locked. He can't touch us.'

We watch the boy slowly back down off our car. His gun is still pointed at us. He never breaks eye contact. He goes to the garbage can, set out on the street for the weekly pick-up, digs through it until he finds a long string of rope. He holds it up for us to see before winding it around his neck. He doesn't pull it tight, just stretches the rope in front of his neck and prances around in front of us.

'When will those police come?' his father groans. We sit quietly watching him. If we move, he may come at us or he may tighten that rope around his neck.

This time it's the police who must take him to the crisis centre. We are too afraid to do so. The police have told us not to. The counsellors have told us not to.

We wait. The five minutes since we talked to the police stretch on and on.

As a young kid, this son wanted to play guitar, so we bought him his first acoustic guitar before he was ten. Knowing what's happened to him — drugs and the counter-culture, the fast fame, the musical genius opening up — I wonder if his father would do it all over. Would he still buy his son that first guitar?

I am just a weary stepmother, the helpmate to this man beside me who must daily face a son who will not go to school. A son who will not go to church. A son who will not obey a curfew. A son who often will not come home on weekends. A son who will not listen to his father.

I have watched his father take him to the school bus and wait until the son boards it. But the school calls later and says the boy never arrived. He just gets off at the next stop. I have watched his father drive him to the school's front door. But the boy walks out the school's back door. Finally, the school sends him to the delinquents' school, but he won't stay there either, so the school district expels him. He has no high school diploma.

What does this boy, this gun-toting, drug-taking boy have? He has a reputation.

I remember the nights when his father and I went to bed to the sounds of this boy practising his guitar. Eight hours, ten hours a day. His finger tips bled. He grew callouses. His hair began to curl around his shoulder blades, then down to his waist. He washed the hair daily, stopped up the shower drain, but refused to comb the curly mass on his head. He started a band.

His father and I went to one of their first gigs. The boys

played about 11 p.m. in a place by the sea. The place advertised: No alcohol. No drugs. No fighting. When the earlier warm-up band left, kids piled into the place to hear our son's band. Inside, we followed the black skirts, the black pants, the black hair, the white faces, the white lipstick. There was a kind of stage with the band – our boy's band – under the lights. The walls of the place were draped in black; a few old benches lined the sides. Kids stood swaying, or moving alone, to the music. I couldn't understand a word of the deafening sound. But the boys sang, tossed their hair, beat their feet, twirled their guitars, threw their drum sticks. And the audience of those hundred kids yelled and screamed and clapped and hooted and hollered and jumped around after each song.

Then our city of 600,000 invited the boy's band to close their prestigious art festival. That's really when his father and I recognised that he and the band were good.

So we went to hear the band close the festival. On the outdoor stage, sound people and light people checked the equipment. The boys took the experience as if they had been on stages like that before. His father and I realised they had. Gigs were coming to them.

The band did a demo tape.

That summer our son called us from New York, a thousand miles away. The band had hitched rides up there. 'We walked into the front office of this record company,' our son told us. 'The secretary tried to kick us out, but we wouldn't go. We looked bad and made noise. She kept trying to throw us out. Then an executive walked in and said, "What's the matter?" We handed him our demo tape and an address in Greenwich Village. Huh! He called us in an hour and asked us to lunch the next day.'

The boy and his band signed with a major record company. His father said, 'That took guts, going to unknown record executives and getting a hearing.' Just teens, the boys set up their own agreement with the record company, signed on without taking much input from adults whom they said, 'don't understand. Don't know about the music business. Can't manage us.'

I remember the meeting the neighbours called at our house to complain about the band's noise.

'I had a garage band when I was young,' the bearded neighbour said. 'I live down this street and I think one hour a day of practice is enough.'

'I hate that grunge sound,' the tall yuppy neighbour said. 'Find somewhere else to practise. This neighbourhood needs quiet.'

'You spook my horse,' the old debutante said. 'My horse needs peace.'

'Okay,' the boy said. 'Our band'll practise one hour a day.' The neighbours went away thinking the boy had listened. But the band only played longer and jacked up the sound louder.

My husband stepped in again. 'You have to finish high school. As long as you take credits, pass courses, you can live with us. If you choose no school, you must move out.'

But to the boy, even the art school was utterly unimportant. He had a record company interested in him. He had an audience, not just a national one. His band's CD came out and critical reviews came from major European countries. The band planned a tour across the United States. School only got in the way.

So the band toured the US, and on the way back, he tried to jump out of a van travelling 60 miles an hour. But no one in the van told his father or me. No one told us how they had missed their gigs on the tour, or if the boys did show up, how often they were late. No one told us about the booze or the drugs or the money or the loss of control in the hotels.

Then the Sunday after the band came home, the band phoned my husband, 'Your son's missing.'

All Sunday the father searched for his son. He called the police. He called all the hospitals. He called the trauma centres. He called the crisis centres. Everyone said the same thing. 'No one like that is here.'

But the next night the state hospital acknowledged that the boy was there. He had tried to kill himself by running in front of a moving van. He only had broken bones, but he was under 24-hour suicide surveillance.

We went to the side of a boy who didn't look like himself, a boy bloated by drugs and pain. After his bones were set, he would spend months in a psychiatric hospital getting his mind back. We watched a boy in diapers who didn't know who he was or where he wanted to be. The diagnosis: depression.

Bipolar disorder they called it later. The suicidal depression happened first, without warning. Then a year later he went into his first manic stage. He talked without breathing it seemed; he smoked without stopping. He didn't sleep for three days. His father took him to the crisis centre. The crisis centre would not take him. He was not a danger to himself or others, they said. So his father and I took him home again.

He didn't sleep for another night. He just kept smoking and doing one-handed push ups. He wouldn't play his guitar. He stared malevolently at his father and me. His eyes grew larger and protruded further and further. We tried again. This time the crisis centre took him. The centre kept the boy stable until he left – to tour Europe.

Now here we are again. This time he is pointing a wooden gun at us and wrapping a rope around his neck.

Finally a white squad car pulls up. The boy stuffs the rope and the gun into the garbage and saunters over to the officer. 'Anything wrong, officer?'

'I'm answering a call.'

The father begins to explain, 'He is making threats and–'

'I'm fine. See, officer, I'm fine. There is NO problem.' He doesn't stumble on his words. 'This is my father. There is NO problem.' Then he jerks a pen from his father's shirt pocket and pokes it at his father.

'What are you going to do with that pen?' asks the officer.

A second squad car drives up.

'Oh. I just wanted to see it. It's my brother who's the problem.'

'Where is your brother?'

'He's in the house. I'll just get him.' The boy walks unhurriedly into the house.

The father says, 'My son punched out the bedroom window. That's why we called you. He's been pointing a wooden gun at us and shaking his fists. He's threatening suicide with a rope.'

The officer asks, 'Why is there glass all over the yard?'

'The boy got mad. He punched out the window.'

Then the officer, six-feet-three, muscles bulging from his shirt, looks around. 'Where is he? He didn't come back from the house. I'm going to see where he is.'

A few minutes later, the cop returns to the group of us standing by the broken glass. 'He's gone. He's not in the house. Must've walked out the other door while we were here talking. We'll look around.'

The cops look on foot for awhile, then ride up and down the streets. 'That kid is a manipulator, isn't he? Well, call us when he comes back.'

Four hours later, the boy returns and lets the police take him to the crisis centre . He knows that he is rocketing into his manic phase.

We've been told that this bipolar condition often strikes older teens and boys in their early twenties. But when the problem first happened to our son, we didn't recognise it as a phenomenon so prevalent it would later be covered in *Time* magazine. Then it was a problem known only to us, to be borne alone. Today we are aware of the causes of bipolar disorders, some hereditary, some not, and understand that the disease is the result of a chemical imbalance. Right now there is no real cure. The boy must take medication, monitor his condition, and seek help when he needs help.

If our son takes his medication and stays away from other drugs, it seems he could be a brilliant musician, if not a genius.

He could have the kind of success written about for stars.

It is up to the boy, the boy alone, to take his medication, to maintain himself, because no one else can live his life for him.

My husband is thin and does not sleep. I refuse to look into the future.

Today, our son is writing the music for his next CD.

And we wait, fearing every time the phone rings. Wary when the doorbell chimes.

Dear Michael

Emma Marx

DEAR MICHAEL,
      (After Adrienne Rich)

Your words today are a *pond where drowned things live*
I want to see raised dripping and brought into the sun.
It's not your face I see, but your father's pain
as he fishes them out, one by one, to find what's lost

a rusted bedspring, a ten-inch shark, a plastic bag.
We fear these words, your father and I,
watch them shimmer wet in the sun and sink back
into brown, heaving water. The murk rises and we wait

for the next reel-in knowing you purposely didn't set
the bait, weren't ready to let up the next load.
We want the night to stalk the pond to force the moon
to pull out your words. You can dazzle the guitar,

find chords for dancers. Find us pathways in this pain.
Or maybe just empty that pond.

The Cuckoo Clock

Anna Bell

It is 11 p.m. on a Saturday and the atmosphere in the house is taut, which is nothing unusual these days. I have retired to bed to write.

I don't know why, but I always knew that the youngest of my three sons was going to give the most trouble. So it has proved. By the age of eight he rarely played after school with friends and often shut himself away in his room. He used to say he was too tired after a day at school to be bothered with anyone. He became quite keen on computer games. I think I justified this solitary occupation with the fact that he was working hard at school so I made excuses on his behalf to mothers when he was invited out to play.

He became stranger over the years. He always seemed to be worried about something. He was very diligent about his school work and would often come and tell me how worried he was about something or other, test marks or deadlines for homework. I seemed to be forever reassuring him that he was doing fine and that everyone was proud of him. He appeared to be continually striving for perfection. I found it very hard to know how best to relate to a child who seemed so sad and solemn and who so rarely smiled. He had a caring family and wanted for nothing so I found his lack of enjoyment and enthusiasm very hard to bear.

One Christmas he asked for a cuckoo clock. It was put on his bedroom wall. Each evening he would pull the chains down to the floor and carefully coil them into two neat little circles. At the time it seemed a harmless enough habit, even though he couldn't settle for the night until this ritual was completed. He also had a shelf of soldiers – each in its precise place – which were not to be touched. He was excessively tidy, but I put that down to the fact that both his parents were tidy. I was quite glad in a way, I suppose. I never had to plead with him to tidy his room like so many of my friends with their children. Nevertheless I became very anxious about it as I was concerned that others might notice these little traits and think them odd. I felt I had given him everything I could and that somehow, if he wasn't happy, then I had failed in some way. That felt like such a huge rejection and I found it very painful.

At about fourteen he began wearing a lot of clothes, maybe two T-shirts under a shirt and two or three pairs of socks. He said he was cold, or more comfortable that way. He would wash his hands a great deal. He would spend at least twenty minutes cleaning his teeth before going to school. It seemed rather eccentric but he justified it on the grounds that he had worn a brace for months and needed to keep his teeth very clean. I accepted his explanations, although I was becoming concerned as his behaviour was beginning to set him apart and I found this frightening.

I took him to Silverstone to watch the British Grand Prix as a birthday treat. It was a very hot day. Not only did he wear two T-shirts, a shirt, a sweatshirt and a leather jacket, he was also, unbeknownst to me at the time, wearing track suit trousers under his jeans, plus the usual three pairs of socks. We sat on the grass and had a picnic and eventually he took off the jacket, but that was all. He didn't feel too well and I don't think he enjoyed the day very much. I certainly didn't – I was too worried about him.

I noticed he was going to bed later and later. He used to say he wasn't tired. I discovered that while no one was around to see him, he was cleaning parts of the house. He would smother the door handles in cleaning stuff. Taps would be smeared and one morning he had cleaned the kitchen floor with what looked like neat Ajax. It was covered in fine white powder.

He would wash clothes that I'd already washed. He liked the machine to run for ages and would never believe that half-load did not mean half-wash. Sometimes, for no apparent reason, when I had done a load of washing and ironing for him, he would say sorry but actually he couldn't use any of it until it had all been done again. He used so many cleaning materials that eventually I had to buy him a supply of his own. I would hide mine, although I knew he would hunt them down if he ran out. That was all right as long as I could remember where I'd hidden things. I found the best place was in a disused dishwasher, but then if I wanted anything I had to make sure he wasn't around to see my secret store. I was becoming as secretive as he was.

It felt like a battle. The more he cleaned the filthier in reality he believed the house to be. And to an extent he was right. He hand-washed his clothes so often that the taps were covered in congealed soap. I wasn't allowed into his room to use the Hoover. His bedroom was thick with dust. He emptied his wardrobe and all his drawers of things he'd collected over the years and put it all into bin liners which were then put in the loft. Clothes were stacked on top of the chest of drawers, together with damp towels because he wouldn't hang his towel in the bathroom. I wasn't allowed to wash any of his bedding and he went for months without changing his sheets.

In the autumn going to school became difficult. He had done brilliantly with his GCSEs getting eleven grades A and

A*. But he was sad and tearful and I would often find little notes saying how sorry he was for making me miserable. Although it was good in some senses that he knew how miserable he was making me, I would usually feel guilty that he carried this extra burden. Somehow, it seemed very inappropriate for a young boy to be so worried about his mother. We were both miserable, and at times it felt as though this misery was all we shared. Often I was consumed with irritation. Some days I would feel suicidal. I was getting up very early and creeping about to steam and press the clothes he wanted dry cleaned. I had come to a special arrangement with the lady at the cleaners. She would bag his clothes for me and I would tell him they'd been cleaned. It was a ten-mile round trip, but the dry cleaning would have cost a fortune otherwise. Sometimes, when time was short, I would find an old bag and try to make it look as though his cleaning had been done.

I was having to unblock the drains several times a week, because he would only dry his hands on loo paper and the toilet was regularly clogged.

Often, if he was very upset about something, he would barricade himself in his room and refuse to come out and I would be convinced he would do something awful to himself. One day in desperation I threatened to break the door down with the axe and actually went to get it from the shed. He just said how awful to have a mad axe woman for a mother. I hated all the subterfuge; the creeping around my own home. I felt trapped and imprisoned and yet my son could be so sweet and considerate. He liked to lie on my bed, hold my hand and chat. We talked about all sorts of things and I tried to develop an interest in things that interested him hoping, I suppose, that the sharing would cheer him up. Thus it was that I began to like the sort of music he enjoyed and we would often play his tapes together. Those were the good times. I felt I was helping him and hoped that perhaps, as if by magic, it would all be better in the morning. But the next day we were always back to square one, with his school books in the freezer. He had previously tried cleaning his books and files with liquid cleaners but he lost a lot of notes that way and his books were soon in a sorry state, so he decided that putting the books in the freezer was the best way he could sterilise everything.

I found myself continually shielding him from the rest of the family. They felt he just needed a clip round the ear, or that he was simply trying to get as much attention as possible. They suggested I ignore him, but I felt too frightened to do that. He seemed so lonely; so isolated. This was a feeling we shared as there were very few people I felt able to confide in. I felt vulnerable. I was desperate to help him and most of my waking thoughts seemed devoted to trying to reach a solution. I became afraid that my family and friends would be angry and irritated with both of us. After all, neither of us was much fun.

Despite my feelings of frustration with him and the sheer complexity of everyday living, I coped because I felt so sorry and anxious for him. I tried so hard not to get angry, but sometimes I found myself yelling at him for being so totally unreasonable and for making my life so difficult. Sometimes he would yell back and so it went on with no end in sight.

One summer we arranged a few days away in a hotel. He was very apprehensive about it and didn't really want to go, but we persuaded him, thinking he'd be all right. He only managed one night, then he asked if we could go home. I made an excuse and we left. We felt angry and he felt guilty. There didn't seem to be anything we could do to make his life happy and remotely normal. It was a dreadful journey home. Silent and gloomy. It felt as though every other family on holiday was having a good time. I felt we somehow stuck out with our major problem.

Then, by chance, I read in the newspapers about a chain of private clinics and their success with obsessives. There was one about fifty miles from us. It was hugely expensive but I arranged for him to be seen by their psychiatrist. Being a private clinic it was nice and clean, a definite plus as far as he was concerned. The psychiatrist was very good and explained to him that he wasn't mad. It turned out that he had been terribly concerned that he would be locked up or put in a straitjacket; that he had known his behaviour couldn't go on, but that he had been frightened of what the outcome would be. The psychiatrist told him that he could still go to medical school and that the problems he'd had would probably make him a better doctor. She assured him that obsession could be cured in time. She pointed out that he was extremely sensitive about what happened to him, his family and the world outside, and that he was unhappy with his appearance. She suggested that he might be afraid of growing up.

He began to see a behavioural therapist once a week who set him tasks and goals to achieve. It was very hard for him. He was not allowed to confide in me, and I was warned not to try to help by reassuring him that what he did was all right. It was very hard for us both. Again I felt a total failure, especially as the therapist was so young. She wasn't even a mother herself. On the one hand I was grateful to her but I also felt upset that she would succeed and cure him where I had so spectacularly failed, despite all my best efforts. I was concerned that I would be judged a poor, or worse, a bad mother. These feelings made me even more guilty. His recovery should be paramount regardless of who brought it about.

He was put on Prozac to relieve the depression. I was very against this at first. It seemed so drastic. A teenage boy needing anti-depressants seemed such an indictment of my parenting ability. I felt even more of a failure as a mother than ever. Eventually I spoke to a pharmacist who told me that it was not addictive and not to worry too much about it. That did help but I found just going to the surgery for the prescription difficult. I felt I was going to be labelled as the mother of that poor boy on Prozac.

After about three weeks the depression began to lift. One of the side effects was tiredness, and he would come home from school and sleep on the sofa for several hours. That worried him. He fretted over the effect on his school work. But now he is beginning to improve. Some days are bad days, although he can do things he couldn't do before and a lot of the cleaning has stopped. It's been a bad day today. He trod in some chewing gum at school, about the worst thing that can happen. He has retired to bed for the rest of the day, and tonight he is still worrying about it.

Some days I truly despair. On others I feel I will cope and that he will turn a corner and recover from this torment that rules his life. And mine.

Why Some Nights I Go To Bed Without Undressing

Elisavietta Ritchie

(For poets Josephine Jacobsen, Rod Jellema, Irene Rouse,
Roland Flint and David and Judy Ray, who lost sons and a
grandson in automobile accidents)

> Even as my children climb
> jungle-gym and pine,
> they too are swinging toward silence.
>
> In desperate dreams I try to save
> my daughter from the flood of night.
> Still she drowns and drowns
>
> while both my sons
> spin nightmare wheels
> against a thundering sky.
>
> This wet midnight terribly awake
> I pace the living room. My youngest son
> is driving his broken Toyota home
>
> from The Grateful Dead Live In Concert.
> The storm keeps pouring over icing streets.
> Finally I go to bed
>
> but toss, alert for doors, or else
> strange strained voices on the phone,
> and I do not undress.

The Wilderness

Caeia March

All my life I was told to fear the wild places. Terrible things lurked there. No child or woman should venture there.

I tried hard to be tame. To stay tame. But wildness will out of a wild woman. I understand that, at last. I am aware of wild landscape around me, wild seascape ahead of me, wild skies above me, wild fires, earth magma, far, far below me. I've tried being tamed and taming myself but I break the bars of every cage I make; and much pain it causes in the process: both the taming and the breaking out.

My sons' adolescent years were partly absorbed by my attempts to be their wild mother and my failures to truly achieve wildness. I failed to protect them from the effects of my unfreedoms – the illnesses and eventual semi-permanent disability which my unfreedoms created. But now I feel that the years of Chronic Fatigue Syndrome were years of a body and soul battling for survival in a world not created for the survival of women like me. Now I am leaving dis-ease behind me – I may not be able-bodied, but I have enough of everything: enough love, enough food, enough shelter, enough warmth, enough friends, enough passionate sex, enough health – a new joy of discovery, waking each morning alive, optimistic and happy.

I used to write of contradictions, as if they were imposed and to be struggled with. Now they clarify. The clouds blow away and the wild skies are revealed; the energy transforms from struggle to gift.

It is the gift of contradiction that creates the knowledge of the self. I am woman of many selves and my sons are a gift: part of self revealing the self. My inner core is mother and lesbian, feminist with sons and I am much wilder now than I was when they were in their teens, more alert and aware of predators, less in need of approval from other women. (I had long since stopped wanting approval from men.) I am more trusting of who I am now; more confident of my voice, my laughter, my mature celebration of me in the world. I have thrown off the secrets, silences and fears. The fear of self falls away and with that, the ability to love grows stronger, because to love someone else you have to honour the self.

I used to write about both my sons, when they were very small – three short stories published and the rest are filed. Then one of them, in his teens, asked me not to. At what point does the man–child silence the woman–mother? At what point does the older woman respect the need of the young ones? Where does equilibrium lie?

About a year ago one of them said, You know that embargo we put on you writing about us? Well, we're adults now, it's fine. You write whatever you like, Mum.

They're so different both my sons. Mark comes with the gift of poetry: he writes and shares it. Trusts. I give him trust in return. Rob comes with the gift of freedom. He demands his. I copy him and learn to demand mine back too. It makes me weep, this loving.

They suffered so badly when they were only nine and seven and I had to leave their father or go mad. I had known for seven years, by then, that I longed to live openly as a lesbian. Having a toddler and being pregnant with the second baby was not the best time to discover my lesbianism. It took me seven years to leave.

I can hardly bear the pain of writing it, nor the guilt of what it did to the little boys. But they are men now and they are fine. It was a long time ago and there has been a lot of loving and a lot of talking, since then. The only gift I had to give them was my honesty. It still is. The truth that I love them and it wasn't their fault.

The whole of their teens was the telling of that truth over and over again. Then, when Mark was nineteen, the summer he finished working on the fruit and veg in Sainsbury's and was due to go, late, to university, he and I went on a hello-and-goodbye trip together to Ireland. We shared a twin-bedded room in each B&B and lived very closely for two weeks. During that time, we ate and walked together, visited museums, rested by the sea, talked to our Irish hosts, found pubs with my maiden name on (I had grown up not knowing that my father had an Irish surname), and we talked and talked and talked.

I am sorry, I said, for all the pain you had when you were nine.

Don't worry, Mum, he replied. It's made me who I am now. It was hard, but I don't regret it.

Years later, it was Rob's turn. He chose The Isles of Scilly. We didn't have such a long visit, though I treasured every minute.

In the interim period, I moved to Cornwall where both of them love to come and stay. Ironically it was the weekend of International Women's Day, when Rob was nineteen, that he suddenly decided he must dash down to see me. He arrived late on the Saturday night and was met by my ex-lover who took him to her place to sleep. I had a house full of women, was living on women's land here in Cornwall and absolutely could not bring a man home at that precise hour. All of us leapt into action in order to meet everyone's needs. On Sunday morning, I stepped over the snoring women lying in sleeping bags all over the living-room floor, kissed my new lover, with whom I was now living in a women-only place, and ran down the lane to meet my younger son. We flung our arms open and held close.

I drove him to the cliffs where we sat above the sea all day talking and re-connecting. He needed me, and when he needed me it was urgent, and I knew it. Of all the weekends when he needed me, that particular weekend was probably the most bizarre. But that's how it happened and our time together was intense and precious.

It was one of those days when a person calls out into the cosmos and asks, Is there anybody there? And, especially, Are you there, Mum?

I need to be needed in that way; and I want to respond. As a mother, that's how I feel.

I thought he might have got someone pregnant. But no. He was just going through a lonely time, a sort of three-am-blues-in-the-middle-of-the-day time.

We walked up through St Loy woods where the light dapples under the trees on to puddles of yellow daffodils in March and shimmers the whole earth blue with bluebells in May. He said there that he'd like to marry, sometime, and that he didn't think he'd look forward to a divorce but, should it happen, to him, he knew he could survive it, because I had, and he knew that his kids would be all right, eventually. He could see that I had found real happiness, he told me, and he said it made him glad.

Being forgiven, by both my sons, is a profoundly healing process.

So, now, this is a wonderful time of life for me. My sons are grown men, aged twenty-four and twenty-two. Together we can story tell those years when, without me, they learned to know me.

I am compelled to write this: every day a gift arrives in my life. Everything comes with a message, image, theme, lesson, picture, motif. It is all wild. There's no time to waste on tameness. If I'm asked to talk on television it's because the magic is working and there's something to learn — some research required that holds a key to a gate to the wild path. If I'm asked to write an article it will be the one that touches the spring on the box of secrets, letting out the secret that's now ready. If I meet a stranger she will be on a journey on the same path for a while. If I make love with my woman lover it will take me to the soft floor of a safe cave in those distant hills. It's all real: and touches me.

It's like coming out again, which I did when my sons were nine and seven. But this time they are men, on their own journeys, centred and calm. There is a lot of love. We have, now that their adolescent years are over, passed through a fire of transformation. Tame mother has become wild mother. They were brave little tigercubs to pass through that fire with me. There were times when I feared they'd run away, back to the known familiar world of their father, never leaving his side again, refusing to come on access weekends, rejecting all I was and might become. But they didn't. Through anguish and turmoil they hung on in there wanting more of me, needing to know me even when I continued to represent unsafety. Were they attracted, too, to the wild places, the places of the soul where, eye to eye we, mother and sons, kept the bond intact?

And I, for my part, could not finally abandon them. I too reached out, reached back, sometimes by looking over my shoulder at them, or with an arm held behind me, my outstretched fingers extended for contact with their fingertips. It was a glad and terrible time, their adolescence.

It's so exciting. Life. Being. Having these people love me. I think it's one of the times I come nearest to understanding unconditional love. Giving and receiving it. Honouring who they are. As people. As adults now. Being loved and respected for me. Myself. Lesbian.

But of course love is never unconditional. The conditions were laid down long ago — I couldn't love them if they experimented on animals; I couldn't love them if they went as mercenaries to South Africa (or anywhere); I'd have a hard time if they joined the police; I'd be very strained if they worked for the DSS!

It's as if, in setting the parameters when they were toddlers/infants, they grew up in the truth of who I was, in so far as I knew that truth.

I don't see them often. Both are in London having finished university. I live in Cornwall. But they chose to come just after New Year in '95, and brought Mark's girlfriend too, all three together because they liked one another. I had said, Not Christmas, because I needed time with my lover. They had said, Not Christmas because they needed time with their Dad and his ageing parents. I had said, I expect you've got friends you want to see over New Year. They said, Yes. Thank God for that, for not making us choose. So they came, when the time was right.

And it was. We ate, walked, talked, played Mah Jong, always Rob's favourite. He was a whizz at maths from being very tiny and he loved all the doubling, and used to win. He always liked to win. We hugged each other. They talked to my lover, Cheryl, and we were family which gave me Mother–Tiger images of a huge cave with a great fire in front of it, warm inside, plenty to eat, no one attacking us.

There was enough attack on all of us in their adolescent years. I crumpled under it with grief and guilt. Frequently, my mother laid the heaviest weights, blaming me incessantly, in large and small ways. At one time, her anger used to lower my resistance to every damn bug that might attack my immune system. That, and trying to face the fact that the lesbian community in general didn't care what I'd done. So I'd left two boys to come out as a lesbian, so what? I had thought they'd be my friends, care, come through. They didn't. As a mother of sons I was in a completely unsafe world just as I had been when I was straight.

It took me a long time to recover from the shock of that. I don't blame them, now. I just hadn't matured enough at thirty-four to realise how much I needed them to support me, praise me, hear me, understand me.

One or two were wonderful. My lover from 1980–86 became a second mother to the boys; taught them to laugh again (we had all forgotten how to laugh); took them on magical mystery tours with theatres and theme parks, woodlands and wombles, ice cream parlours and Brixton cafes. My lover from 1986–1992 said she'd be their grown-up friend and was steadfastly there for them. She is still their friend and it was she who met Rob at the station when I had a houseful of women. Both those ex-lovers were lesbians whose ability to give and receive love was nurturing for my children, as they grew into teenagers, and supportive for me, when I failed many times to be the strong woman I longed and tried to be.

Facing failure isn't easy. It takes courage because once you've faced it, you have to overcome it if you want to survive. Eventually my body gave in, caved in, and turned itself inside out. I crawled into bed lost somewhere inside a sobbing, shaking exterior. The diagnosis of ME was a relief. I had thought I had gone mad, right off the edge.

With a damaged immune system following glandular fever, I was in no fit state to deal with my guilt, my grief, or my devastation at living without my children. Struggling with low income, and living with nosy, noisy, and occasionally violent neighbours, I became sick in my soul, sad at my broken dreams. I longed for a bright new peaceful life.

My sons, as teenagers, saw me like that. No energy, lack of sleep, words falling through holes in my head, words leaving my mouth too fast, torrents of words that I couldn't catch up with. Legs that wouldn't walk, muscles that wouldn't hold me up, hands that dropped and spilled and broke things, ears that couldn't stand the slightest noise, lungs allergic to benzene and traffic fumes, skin that came out in weird rashes. For several months there was also agrophobia – if the milkman left the bottle on the path instead of the doorstep it stayed there all day till someone else brought it in.

But the will to live is strong in a wild woman. It's the same will that runs in the DNA in those small patches of wild grass that insist on growing up through tarmac.

During those years I wrote my way to freedom. However, for the first two years of ME, I couldn't physically hold a pen. I videoed my third novel, *Fire! Fire!*, in my head while I was lying in bed.

Then, later, I allowed my high-tech friends to persuade me that what I needed was a word processor to help with my disability. It did. I was sorry that I had taken so long to be dragged reluctantly into the late twentieth century! I caught up with my inner world of video-film, completed the novel and collapsed again.

Then the call of the wild came strongly. Leave the city. Your body is dying here. Your soul is dying. Come to me. Come to me.

I talked to my sons who were at that time aged fourteen and sixteen.

Go for it, said Robert.

I can just see you in green wellies, Mum, said Mark.

They loved me, which was unbelievable but true. I couldn't see much rational reason for it, but I think they had heard me answering that call in whimper sounds softly for years. Go for it, they said.

One day, said Rob on the phone last year, I'd like a wife and kids and to live in Cornwall. I was rendered speechless. That tiny baby with whom my self seemed bonded at the hip, who had always laughed with me and wanted to be with me, fancied a life near me, near the wild soul places. For this is an ancient landscape which knows how to take care of itself: you can't build on the cliffs, because your house would fall down a mine shaft, so the coast path remains alive here, give or take the tramping feet of tourists.

You can stay here with me and J–, said Mark when I needed to come to London. It's a studio flat.

Won't she mind? I asked, realising we'd all be sleeping in the one room on two sofa beds.

No. I'll ask her. But she won't mind.

Unbelievable but true. So I returned to London, as a visitor, and I was so happy there. One evening, I had dinner with both sons and my best friend, Penny. My sons love her. They met her the same day as I did, outside the school gates, and we have been laughing together since then. There's nothing she doesn't know about me. She is straight, strong and stroppy. Easily a match for all of us, singly or together. She loved me and my boys thoroughly and took them before and after school for a year when I left them with their father so that I could come out as a lesbian. Throughout their teens she was their friend, who loved them.

I'm glad it's now, not then. Some of it was awful. But some of it was funny, too. Like the time when me and the boys went to look for a place in the Isabella plantation in Richmond Park so that they'd know where to scatter my ashes.

Unperturbed by the seriousness of the situation – after all I'd been at death's door several times, as they well knew, and seemed to have a very determined life force that always rallied round – they debated between themselves what to do if I popped my clogs when it was snowy on the ground.

Well, said Rob, we'd have to put her in an urn on the mantelpiece till the snow melted.

We'd better make sure we didn't knock it off, then, replied Mark. Or she'd end up on the hearth rug and then we'd have to Hoover her up again.

Yes, said Rob, turning to me. You wouldn't like that would you, Mum? I mean, you'd end up in the Hooverbag with all the fluff and dried up baked beans and stuff.

They grabbed me by the hands, and we skipped, laughing and singing, all the way up through the azaleas, and I had a glimpse, then, of the wild woman who was never going to be lined up in a row of armchairs in someone else's 'home' watching someone else's telly and with the radio on in the other corner.

I don't need the azalea plantation any longer, nor even a notion of where my ashes will be scattered. I am leaving all that pain and dis-ease behind me, here in this landsea and moonsky place, where I am alive and healing and finding peace.

Last autumn, I went with Cheryl to stay with my sister in the north and to see my mother. I had healed so much by then. I had so much love in my life that I didn't need any extra. I no longer needed my mother's approval. Instead, I simply wanted to make peace. And, it seems, so did she. Faced with Cheryl and me together, my mother had to recognise my newly found inner calm. I thought to myself, if she can die happy, I can live happy. I had let go of the need for anything else, when I went to face the grandmother of my two sons.

When I fell in love with Cheryl, I was deep in bitter childhood memories. She was leaving a marriage and grieving for her first woman lover who had left. We'd been friends for three years and I had no idea we would fall in love.

This is now our fifth summer; and we have been here living together in this rented house on the cliffs for almost a year. We have given a great deal of our time to learning new language patterns and ways of sustaining our creativity within an intense lover relationship, for we are both writers with hefty schedules and busy lives.

The wide windows here face towards the ocean and give me a sense of magical reality because in my second novel I included a little granite house on the cliffs between Pendeen and St Ives. I called it Hermit's Hut and gave it wide windows that overlooked the Atlantic.

I dreamed for years of leaving the city and living in a place like this. I used to wonder if it was a fantasy, which was scary because fantasies can never become reality. It's dreams that can be made to come true. But you have to dream them first.

I search the ocean's vast empty space. You have to be living here with your body NOT inside out or you'd dissolve into this ocean and never be seen again. You need your skin on the outside where it belongs, your heart intact, not full of nails or broken glass, and your soul glad, empowered full of Wild Self. So, I tell my sons that I am mother, lesbian, whole unto myself. They know it and they love me for it. It frees them to learn who they are: to dare to be. Loving them has been an amazing story, and this is still an amazing life.

I always wanted children – from the age of thirteen I knew that I wanted to be a mother. I had the flu and I sat in bed holding an antique teddy bear that came down from my cousin. I felt its hard, bald head against me, and I had a womb lurch and realised that one day I dreamed of holding a new-born child of my own like that. At that time, 1959, lesbianism was so invisible in the media and in everyday life that I had absolutely no way of associating lesbianism with myself nor lesbianism with mothering, so my inner knowledge – that I wanted children – masked my lesbianism from me for years.

Today I live with an amazing woman-lover in a rented house on the Cornish cliffs; I have two grown up sons, whom I dearly love; and I know that it is not indulgent for a woman to dream. It is absolutely skin-shavingly, life-savingly crucial.

There's a dream woman living happily inside me, who will go on reaching out to her sons; a wild and happy woman here on the edge of the wilderness.

The Roller Coaster

Carole Arnold

It is hard to know where to begin. Perhaps at the very beginning. The mothering of adolescents must surely start with the invariably painful process of giving birth to them as babies. And it doesn't get any better!

The emergence of raw new life is traumatic, uncomfortable, painful and exhilarating for both mother and child. When I see a birth, I weep. Whether I weep with the emotion of the moment or in some secret empathy with the ignorant but happy victim who is cradling to her breast the would-be source of her future joy and pain, I do not know.

At about twelve or thirteen years of age, in my opinion, the entire birthing cycle begins again. This end of childhood heralds the slow birth of adulthood through the process of adolescence. Even the lengthiest of births is guaranteed to be over in a day or two, but this process can, and does, last for years – an eternity and a half for us, as mothers and carers. Maybe not always hell, but certainly for the most part, sheer purgatory.

My qualifications for sharing my thoughts on this subject are: I am a mother of adolescents, a foster mother of adolescents, an adoptive mother and would-be adopter, and I work with adolescents who are at risk either to society or to themselves – and sometimes to both. These experiences have helped me realise that I do not understand adolescents at all. So if you are reading this hoping to gain a great and significant insight into understanding youth, forget it! What I have to offer is a mish-mash of despair and hope, pain and joy, usually experienced either together or in quick succession to each other.

I expect that, if I were to be analysed, somewhere deep inside my psyche, a deep-rooted current of masochism would be found. Perhaps I relish the role of martyr, which mothering, working, caring for and loving adolescents allows me to fulfil almost endlessly? I do not know myself what the truth is. Why do I fill my life, my mind and my home with human beings who, involved in their own painful discovery of pushing their way into the world of adulthood, are not aware of, or even recognise the needs and often the very existence of others around them?

I do not mean to be completely negative. Often I enjoy their company and their personalities immensely. Otherwise I could self-diagnose masochism immediately!

I often find myself liking and admiring the very honesty which irritates me. As civilised adults we smile at those we secretly wish would shut up and go away, talk politely with people we hate and despise. Adolescents do not. They are truthful in their opinions and wishes. If I irritate an adolescent I will be told to 'go away' or ' fuck off'. A conundrum. The very quality which I admire in them, I attempt to alter and refine. I also enjoy their capacity of deviousness and ingenuity which they use to extract money, conditions and terms for co-existence. Their sense of business acumen and imagination if used in industry would ensure many a millionaire. If I was repaid the money 'borrowed' from me over the years, I too would be incredibly wealthy. I enjoy the rich diversity of excuses for not arriving home at the requested time. From the mundane to the priceless, have been the broken-down bus and loss of bus fare home (only a one, I'm afraid here!), to being chased by a man with an axe (a nine, I really enjoyed that one!).

For approximately the last ten years of my life I have been involved in the world of adolescents, involved in the mysteries of pre-menstrual tension; hair growth in an assortment of places – some desired, some not desired – hence my husband shaving his face with a razor full of leftover leg hairs; voices deepening and rising to match rising (or risen) sexual and hormonal urges. I live with tears and tantrums, screaming and swearing, doors being banged and kicked, shouting and sulks.

My house smells of pizza and joss sticks. It is filled with a medley of jungle, heavy metal, rap and soul, love songs, pop and jazz emitted from a plethora of sources simultaneously. All this I now regard as normal life. Indeed quietness, solitude and peace are achievable only in the bath or in bed – and these places are not always sacrosanct. Or before eleven o'clock on a Sunday morning. When they do not have to rise for school, or college, or work, adolescents bear a strong resemblance to vampires – only venturing out in the hours of darkness and sleeping through daylight. Perhaps I should hang some garlic on the bathroom and bedroom door when I'm in there!

I have a series of questions about the deeper mysteries of life revolving around my existence with adolescents, which have, as yet, to be answered.

Why are empty milk bottles and orange juice cartons put back in the fridge and not thrown out? Why are all the chocolate biscuits purchased on Saturday, eaten before Monday morning? Why is it, despite having asked beforehand, that when I go into the bathroom for a bath, the world and its dog want to come in and get something? Why is there no loo roll or shampoo left when I go to use them? Why is there always only the bread crusts left in the plastic bag in the afternoon, even though I bought the loaf that day? Why is it only me that throws these same crusts into the bin? Why are there always wet towels on the floor of all their bedrooms and none in the bathroom? Who dumps mugs, with interesting green mould growing inside them, in the kitchen?

I have lived through the pain of school, college and university examinations and the strains of waiting for the subsequent results. I have visited an assortment of police stations in my capacity as 'appropriate adult' and waited apprehensively for the magistrates' decisions to charges brought to court. I have supported young people through drug-induced 'trips' and the sickness of too much alcohol. I have endured (barely) the agonies and the pleasures of first love (as well as the second, third, fourth, etc., etc.); acne and menstruation; the joys and traumas of friendship; the passing of driving tests; the fear and realities of pregnancy and the choices thereafter. Triumphs and sadness; joy and utter despair. Often as I share the events so I share the emotions. I have felt my palms sweat, my heart beat faster as they have opened examination results, or put the litmus paper into the sample of a home testing pregnancy kit. I have wept at the loss of a child – wanted and unwanted – and felt bereft and unhappy because a relationship has ended.

Their capacity for touching the extreme depths and heights of any emotion is as great as the pendulum swing of their moods. Extreme joy which touches all who come into contact with it can be followed, in the blink of an eye, by utter and total despair. Sometimes anger. Even to make eye contact in such circumstances can and will be seen as an act of hostile aggression. From being their friend and mentor is a short intake of breath from being their enemy.

To try to understand, to attempt to make sense of what is happening between myself and them, therein, I truly believe, lies real madness. To support them in achieving their chrysalid change in order that they can grow and develop and realise their own possibilities is what I strive for. In reality, I shout and swear and scream and sulk and remain totally baffled by their actions like every other adult I know. My eldest daughter once complained that I showed her little of the understanding which I displayed to complete strangers. I told her that I could give her understanding or I could be her mother. I couldn't do both!

Perhaps I also enjoy them because of the sheer power of their emotions and lifeforce. Their feelings, even when I am not intimately involved with them, are so tangible, so strong, they can almost be tasted on the tongue – both sweet and bitter. There is a lifeforce in them which is unquenchable and unstoppable. I firmly believe that if supported they can achieve what even they believe to be impossible. I enjoy helping them discover what is possible, to witness their realisation that their potential is greater than they ever thought. What I do not enjoy, what makes me suffer, is their pain, their anger which is passed on, transferred, often to myself. Mothers and carers become the 'whipping boy' for their adolescents' turmoil.

I have worked with and lived with, teenagers, whom I have loved, liked, disliked, admired and only just tolerated. In the beginning, I was consumed with guilt if I acknowledged any feelings other than caring ones, for these young people. Now, I freely acknowledge that they have the same abilities as adults to elicit in me a variety of responses which includes dislike. I have stopped feeling guilty about these feelings. Well almost!

And when they hurt, like primitive animals they know how to go for the jugular. They know my soft spots, my weaknesses, my buttons to press, for reaction. And they are often as careless with feelings, with love, as they are with their possessions. If something is broken – throw it away – replace it. For with the young, nearly everything is replaceable. They live in a throwaway society. They expect that I as an adult will forgive them whatever they do to me. They test and drive me to unreasonable limits and are upset or annoyed if their motives are questioned. But however logical I am in understanding and acknowledging their actions when they hurt me, I have found that it does not stop or even salve the pain. And yet this is something else I attempt to teach them – that it is better to feel hurt and experience pain than to shut down on emotion!

I know that I, too, am unreasonable, often, in my demands of them. I hate to see their talents thrown away or underused and I feel compelled to push them further, to achieve for themselves what is, perhaps, more than is reasonably possible for them to imagine. I do not know what differences I have made to the young people whose lives I have touched and come into contact with. I know they have exasperated and tired me; hurt and angered me. But I also know that they have sometimes allowed me to care for them and to watch them emerge from their cocoon of confused adolescence into independence and maturity.

Caring for, loving, supporting and 'mothering' adolescents is like being carried on a roller coaster. All I can do is hang on each time and hope that when the ride finishes I am still in one piece to enjoy the end!

Surviving the Teenage Years: Notes from a Grandmother

Isobel

There is life after teenage. Hard to believe when you're facing a screaming virago or sullen, resentful stranger. You are now a fallen idol. From Mum! who could put everything right, you have become Mum! who understands nothing.

Before you throw in the towel, or leap from the bedroom window, or throw your offspring out of the door, find a quiet moment. And consider.

Your child has stepped into a world beyond your reach. The rules, customs, clothes and hairstyles are not within the scope of your experience. Pressures and temptations increase with each decade.

Our teenagers are troubled. They are uncertain. They are emotionally insecure. They are worried about future unemployment, by the continued demolition of their world, by pollution, by the threat of nuclear war. Our teenagers do think, and where rational thought fails to provide solutions, they *feel*. Add to this their burgeoning sexuality, the cynical targeting of youth by the advertising world, and our teenagers are confused and vulnerable.

This is your final and most demanding role as a parent as your children struggle to stand on their own two feet. As a grandmother, here are my tips for survival.

Firstly, I believe that guidelines are still necessary, for your own peace of mind, and to provide your children with a sense of security. But make them flexible.

Talk as one adult to another. Ask for advice sometimes. If you have faith in their opinion — they will too.

Stick to what matters. Teenagers can be rude, fault-finding, arrogant, aggressive and illogical. But try not to become the Opposition. If you turn a blind eye to the vagaries of fashion, then they may listen when what they wear borders on the obscene. Avoid confrontation over the trivial. Avoid confrontation altogether if it's at all possible. Thick make-up, dyed hair and a shaved head are not permanent. A row about drugs will have no impact if last week you raved about purple eye shadow.

It is hard to love a teenager in the full flow of their tantrums but it does not last forever. Be supportive. As their self-confidence grows, you will understand that all the hassle was nothing to do with what *you* did or said. They are human fledglings trying out their wings. Look on it as necessary, nest-leaving behaviour.

You will both survive, you and your teenager. Ask your own mother.

Mothering the Rebel Female

Elizabeth Fraser

Daughters, daughters. I am blessed with two of them. One is nineteen and unemployed. She has pale skin, fine blonde hair, seven standard grades (O levels) one higher (A level) and a boyfriend with dreadlocks. The other is fifteen and a reluctant but so far persevering schoolgirl. She has long red hair and is currently on a brave quest for a sensitive, communicative boyfriend with or without dreadlocks. Neither of them have any idea of what they want to either 'do' or 'be'. So far, they only know what they don't want to 'do' or 'be' and I am sick of people asking me that stupid question.

They have me, a single-parent Mum, also unemployed. I trained as a therapist, published some writings and started my own business but I'm still not making any money. And just for the record I do have a boyfriend who has a heart big enough for all of us and the good sense not to live with us. Not too far away is their interfering granny, another red-head (once) who has always been neurotic but now borders on the psychotic.

She really is quite deluded, but she's 'ours'.

I always gave my daughters everything I possibly could; 'spoilt them' my Mum said, but what did she know about growing up in the 'comparative poverty' of Thatcher's Britain? When they were little they did not compare and I protected them as long as I could from the unsatisfactory truth of our dependence on the State. Materially speaking, my 'spoiling' them did not amount to much. Doing everything for them became my main way of giving. During their childhood we lived in rented cottages in isolated rural Scotland. I never scrimped on food and we had to have a car; apart from that there was no money. I definitely played the self-sacrifice game. They had a full social life with their schoolfriends. I had none. I was cook, cleaner, nurse, chauffeur, etc. I became invisible. They were the future and their needs came first.

What a fool I was. Why didn't somebody tell me that as a woman, mothering girls, it is not what you give them or do for them that counts in the long run? It is who you are and how you feel about yourself that matters. *You* are their role model. This is a disturbing thought which puts self-sacrifice in a macabre new light. Women perpetuating their own unsatisfactory roles.

My own fragile self-image is reflected in my daughters. The elder in particular is, on the surface, feisty and somewhat arrogant, but just below that she is hurt and angered by what she perceives to be the injustices of her life and afraid of the effort it is going to take to overcome them. This insecurity, anger, hurt and fear must be what turns one child into a rebel and not another. This is why my friends' daughters are cycling on Arran while mine are 'tripping' at Glastonbury.

It seems to run in families. I was an extremely rebellious teenager, shaking off my mother's shallow expectations. Seeing humanity hurtling towards its own destruction, I rejected the 'channelled into industry' education on offer and the 'safe' career options and chose an alternative path. Or so I thought at the time. Actually, what I ended up doing was being a mother and running a home, not very alternative at all. Then, when my children were six and three years old, my marriage failed, and we fell neatly into one of this country's poverty traps, becoming a single-parent family.

There was very little discipline in our house. Looking back I know this was a mistake. I did not know how to stand up for myself nor how to set limits and boundaries without feeling like a tyrant. I was not going to repeat the inconsistent and petty rules forced on me as a child. I desperately wanted to avoid confining my daughters or moulding them; I wanted to encourage, praise and nurture them so that they would grow into brave, healthy, proud and strong-willed women, sensitive sisters, creative free spirits.

When my elder daughter reached early adolescence, we moved to a council house in town. I knew the girls would need to separate from me and I thought that this new urban environment would allow it to happen. It was as though I was saying 'here you are, you can rebel too, you can find some solidarity, you can experiment with sex, drink, smoking and drugs, just like I did.' I saw it as inevitable. I steeled myself for more self-sacrifice. I would be even more invisible, have less money and a lot less sleep! Less satisfaction too, for these bright, happy wholesome little girls were fast becoming disenchanted. Adolescent unhappiness led rapidly to low self-confidence and self-destructive habits. Did I set it up? In expecting it, did I collude with it? I will never know. And I am left with the useless old question, 'what could I have done differently?'

My gentle graceful eldest became a moody 12-13-year-old, holding herself apart from me, blaming me for many things. She started smoking and nearly drank herself to death one night with a bottle of spirits kept under the sink for cleaning purposes. At 14 she was 'going out' with the school's drug dealer, a likeable but far-too-old-for-his-years 15-year-old hell-bent on getting out of his mind. It is quite admirable, looking back, how she managed to join in and keep school together at the same time. He was expelled and she went on to raves, drinking with her pals, Ecstasy, speed.

At 16 she went to live with her American father for a year. (This absent father is, of course, a large but hidden part of this story.) While she was there she picked up some serious drug habits, daily dope smoking and wild acid trips. She returned looking like Madonna gone wrong. Bleached hair, white skin, black lips, giant pupils, skinny body, American drawl. After a few days at home, reality hit her. She was disappointed in her father and felt worse about herself. She cried a lot.

Meanwhile, her sister had her own problems. She was being bullied at school and was conducting her own personal experiments in the humiliation and degradation of sexual encounters with the male adolescent. Pretty soon, she too turned to drinking and drugs. It is so prevalent here in this small town, so 'normal' that I rebuke myself for expecting anything else.

Recently, after a few weeks of unsuccessful job hunting, my beloved elder daughter went on a drinking binge, spending her nights in the pub, the one that closes its doors with everyone still in it. The one that harbours all the addicts and the alcoholics. It attracted her, this pit of despair and despondency. She wanted to try it out. Her boyfriend left her. Seriously worried about her, I tried to confront her. She told me that she was a bit of a piss-head at the moment, and that I just had to accept it. I thought about my choices. I am not the kind of parent who throws hysterics and throws her child out. All I could do was cry and tell her she was frightening me.

A few weeks before her 15-year-old sister had severely upstaged her. She too decided to visit 'Dad' and came back looking like a leftover from Woodstock. She drank on the train from the airport till she passed out, missed her stop and ended up hysterical and very distressed at Glasgow Central. She was 'put' on the next train home and would have missed her stop again had we not searched the train for her. 'Is "that" what you are looking for?' sneered the guard. Slumped in the last seat, semi-conscious, reeking of booze and wearing a vomited-over Magic Roundabout T-shirt was my adored youngest child who is not even fully grown yet. Her hands are still pudgy, her 'my little ponies' are still in the jumble box in the hallway; and her sweet innocence is still all I see.

Yesterday I came home from a trying afternoon with my mum. My daughters had done the dishes and the washing and were laughing, smoking marijuana and playing Monopoly. This was a good day. This looks like harmless fun. My mission as a mother has been to give to my daughters the love and the freedom that my parents could not or would not give to me – their love was conditional. To a certain extent I have succeeded in this mission. I love my daughters no matter what. But a mother's love is not enough and freedom does not fit well into the structure of our society.

How could I give my daughters the security and stability of a place in the world or the self-discipline to create what they want to achieve in life when I did not have any of this myself? All I have bestowed is the capacity to live without these things. I had not bargained for this atmosphere of hopelessness and despair which they are soaking up like sponges. It is bigger than all of us and being young and only human they are numbing their bright minds and confused feelings in whatever ways they can.

I am depressed by all of this, numbed by it. My anger has no place to go. I nourish my daughters back to health in between the bouts of self-abuse and wonder why I bother. I am always here and yet I dream sometimes of running away. I don't need this. This is hell.

'Don't exaggerate, Mum, we're only having fun'; and 'There is nothing else to do,' they cry. Is this true? I think of all the days they sleep through. Long bright sunny ones. I think of all the local events they are too hungover to go to or national ones they could be inspired by. No, they are set in their ways like old people, they do the same thing day after day, week after week. They stay in bed until the afternoon, then stomp around in bad moods until they have enough tea, tobacco, sugar, food, etc. in their systems. Then they go out and find somewhere to get wasted and do nothing; or they simply stay in to get wasted and do nothing.

My lack of authority leaves me feeling trampled on. I don't know how to protect myself from this, how to keep some stress-free space. I relied on powers of persuasion when they were younger, a skill that they have long since surpassed me in. Sometimes I withdraw my sympathy and understanding and become mopey and sullen myself. I leave the housework and become depressed. The urge to run away is strong but I don't; I know the urge will pass.

I am grateful for the wisdom that has come with middle age. If I want oblivion I can soothe myself with country walks or immerse myself in a good book. But whatever happens, I am determined stay with it, stay present. I will never escape into the pathetic deluded old age of my parents' ostrich generation. I love my daughters and, even though they push me to my limits all the time, I have to keep the channels of communication open and have faith that eventually they will come out of this self-destructive phase. I hope this is not my particular form of delusion.

Will they pull through? The Mother in me is deeply concerned for them. Particularly for my fragile eldest daughter. She is wise and sensitive enough to see the mess she has inherited but not confident enough to feel able to change things. She is stuck. I see this and am unable to help her. I suffer watching her.

Both my daughters are peace-loving, artistic. They are not materialistic nor acquisitive. They accept our poverty with stoicism and are endlessly caring of their friends and of those less fortunate than they. Okay, so they take me and their home comforts for granted. Some would say that is abusive to me. But whose fault is that? It is mine. Their rebellion hurts no one more than it hurts and damages themselves.

I have high hopes for these two daughters of mine; hopes that they will be able to give full creative expression to their unique and precious hearts and minds. These hopes are partly fired by my own frustrated hopes and visions. I could be repeating my own mother's selfish expectations. I realise that my daughters may well drop out of society without ever truly being in it just like I did. In all likelihood they will become mothers themselves and start the whole blessed thing all over again. I accept that fact and continue to love and support them no matter what they do or who they become, and I console myself that they are, at their age, far more in a state of becoming than I am.

Bake a Cake

Helena Hinn

Kirsty wouldn't eat my food. Oh no. Any food I placed in front of her, however enticing it was, she would push out of the way with force.

For I was the wicked stepmother who was trying to poison her with the blood red apple of jealousy. But the jealousy was, in fact, in her heart. It had gnawed away at her like a dirty maggot.

For two years this continued.

Then, one Saturday, as I was spearing the hearts out of lime-green cooking apples (a suitable action for a wicked stepmother, don't you think? – to spear the hearts out of young growing things, and one substantiated by literature and fairy tales), Kirsty approached me.

'Apple cake', she demanded.

'Actually, it's baked apples today,' I replied.

'No, we're making apple cake,' she decided with the determination I knew so well.

So we baked an apple cake. Together. We folded the wholemeal flour, flakey, into the sticky fat and dark sugar. We lacerated the Bramleys into moist cubes and floated them in viscous mixture. Our hair met over the earthenware bowl.

And so it was as we welded the cake, *we* welded together — a stepdaughter and a stepmother without shared blood, but with shared experiences.

Daughter in Deep, Deep Water

Diana Scott

Parenting was something I was determined to do better than my own parents. I could hardly have done worse. I had grown up in a so-called dysfunctional family, which had left four of its five children deeply scarred by abuse and one dead by suicide at the age of twenty.

But family patterns are hard to break and, although I had a lot of therapy several years after my sister's suicide, I still brought to parenting my unresolved fears. Perhaps my children picked up on this because they tested me to the limits. Both my children have been 'difficult', one from birth, and the other during adolescence. What could I have done to produce such vipers in the nest? What was it about my lifestyle that had unleashed such anger in my children?

Like other mothers with broken relationships, I blamed myself. I brought up my daughter, Rosie, by myself for the first six years of her life. I couldn't have wished for a happier, more agreeable daughter. Then I moved in with Phil, who was a few years older than myself, and we had Craig. Craig was from the very start an agitated and demanding child who screamed interminably. Life was mostly hell. Phil left when Rosie was thirteen and Craig was seven. A year later Dave moved in with us. My children experienced two fathers, in Rosie's case two stepfathers.

Sociologists tell us that, statistically, step-families have a very high chance of breaking down. I can certainly attest to the sheer horror of trying to rear kids with stepfathers who seemed unable to weather the emotional maelstrom that their arrival brought.

When Rosie reached adolescence, her first stepdad had just waltzed off the scene and another was looming on the horizon. I was in a rather dilapidated state emotionally and, as Rosie entered the teenage years, my formerly sweet, compliant daughter transformed slowly into a disdainful, sulky, mutinous person who seemed to hate me and everything I stood for. She showed this through frequent bouts of swearing at me, denouncing me contemptuously; or by completely ignoring me. There were some light moments, but Rosie's predominant mood was one of cold anger. She was pulling all the usual teenage stunts, but in megadoses. My attempts to communicate with her – and I tried several different tacks – were met at best with a scornful sneer, at worst with 'Fuck off, cunt-features.'

I understood the change in Rosie's behaviour in terms of the domestic changes which had come at a time when she most needed stability. It was plain to me that the loss of her stepfather had taken its toll; and that had been compounded by the death of my father. Her granddad had been the most solid constant male presence in her life and she adored him. But my awareness of these influences did not make my own task any easier.

We had little contact with Rosie's father who, by this time, had become a heroin addict. I couldn't talk to my own mother, who was in a state of mourning for my father and was herself slowly drifting towards death. And Rosie reserved her aggressive nastiness for me, so her school believed that I was exaggerating the problem or that I couldn't deal with normal teenage turbulence. I was completely isolated and unsupported. Alone in the front line.

Rosie's often horrendous behaviour and the consequent pain and distress were made worse by my unrealistically high ideals. I wanted the perfect relationship with my daughter. I yearned to stay close to her in a way I had never experienced with my own mother. The precious empathic bond I had had with her until the teenage years was vanishing and I found that very hard to bear.

At the age of fourteen Rosie had her first period. I had envisaged creating a beautiful space for her to mark her blossoming into womanhood. So I organised, with other women, a celebration for her and some of her friends. We met in a springtime birch wood all dressed in red. We had a sauna together, throwing our bodies into the clear water of a nearby loch to cool down. The older women massaged the young women, then led them back to a feast that we had laid out amongst a circle of snowdrops and red candles. We gave each of the young women a gift and shared our experience of bleeding.

Yet I scolded Rosie when she didn't change her sanitary towel and her new white trousers were stained. The raw distress which surrounds menstruation, transmitted to me by my own mother, had me in its stranglehold. I failed to put myself in the place of a young woman on her first day of bleeding with no idea of just how much blood to expect and how best to deal with it.

On other occasions I found myself going overboard with a furious force that she didn't deserve. Like when she first shaved her legs. She was about thirteen. We were swimming at a local loch with women friends. I had always impressed on her the folly of shaving legs and when I spotted that she had done precisely that, I chased her round the loch ranting. Did she want to become a doll, consigned to shaving her legs every few days and wasting her precious energy? I was furious and it took me some time to calm down. This was the first time she had taken a step to separate herself from my values and, although she had been pouring scorn on them for a long time now, I had believed that was all talk. I felt threatened. I felt that I was losing my daughter to the patriarchs.

I remember her blockading herself into the bathroom, plastering on pancakes of make-up before she went to school. Her beautiful fresh face was converted into a sickly synthetic mask. I harangued her, made her wash it off, but she applied it again at school. I backed off when my common sense told me that my approach was counterproductive. I also glimpsed that my own reaction contained strong feelings of self-blame — I had not succeeded in raising my daughter with enough self-esteem to value her face as it was. At an intellectual level, I acknowledged the pressures on girls to conform to sexist images of womanhood, but I felt I should have been able to counter them and that I had failed.

At times, I wished I could treat Rosie like Rapunzel and keep her safe in her tower. At other times I experienced her experimenting with different images as an essential stage in dealing with newly emerging sexual feelings. I had been brought up in a village stronghold of Calvinism and I suspect that the 'sexual revolution' of the sixties couldn't eradicate in me a kneejerk ingrained fear of explicit sexual expression. I watched Rosie discard her couldn't-care-less outfits for dresses that Mae West might have felt were going a bit far. Whilst admiring Rosie's flamboyant display of emergent sexuality, like most mothers, I also feared for her. After initial angry bouts with her over the leg-shaving and the make-up, however, I learnt to relax my attitude.

But the torrent of contempt poured on me continued. For the most part, I remained patient and affectionate. There were times, of course, when the abuse took its toll and I battled not to respond in kind. It took a huge effort not to unleash venom back at her. But there were things that were harder for me to deal with than outright nastiness – things which demonstrated to me that Rosie was deeply upset and that I had to make allowances for her.

I heard through the parental grapevine that she was drinking quite heavily. Once, when she was thirteen, she pulled a cupboard down on herself and passed out. In the evenings, she wouldn't return from discos at the times we had agreed, and I would anxiously patrol the streets with visions of her in a drunken stupor, easy prey for the passing rapist. One New Year's Eve, at a party in a big house, I lost track of her for a couple of hours. A male friend told me he had seen her dead drunk and then later being 'humped', as he put it, in a public place by a heavy-looking man. He told me how sad he felt for Rosie.

I was flooded with horror, guilt, and fear. My daughter was going off the rails. She was thirteen, and probably having unprotected sex with guys who were just using her. But she hotly denied the reported event. I tried reasoning with her about her safety. But she resorted to climbing out on the roof in the middle of the night, crawling down on to a wall and hitching alone in the dark to the nearest town. The situation was getting out of hand.

So I made a joint appointment for us with a Clinical Psychologist called Andrew. We only saw him three times together and a couple of times separately. It was excruciating for me. Rosie unleashed fresh depths of hatred and contempt for me in front of him. I felt totally exposed. I felt an inadequate mother, a complete failure. Andrew was a rather handsome caring man, and part of me badly wanted to impress him. But there was no chance of that.

Yet this public purging, the exposure of her feelings towards me, seemed to have a positive effect on Rosie. Slowly, things began to improve. And whilst my pleas for her safety had fallen on deaf ears, Rosie listened to Andrew. She started to turn up at the agreed rendezvous at the agreed time after a night out.

She stopped her solo midnight excursions. The drinking seemed to settle down into a more normal teenage pattern. And drugs, which I knew she took now and again, didn't seem to take over her life. There were still the splurges of animosity towards me and the usual teenage untidiness and selfishness. But, gradually, things eased up. There were even times when we laughed and had fun together. She and her gang of girls, infectiously giggling away together, buffered us through bad times. I enjoyed watching them spend a frantically gleeful three hours getting ready to go out on the town, tossing off one dress, trying one hairstyle after another, amidst shrieks of mirth.

Things had reached a more even keel when Rosie left home at sixteen to do a Youth Training in Horsemanship. She was dead keen to leave home. She had the talent to go to art college but didn't want to. I felt I had failed to give her the confidence needed to tackle the academic work required. Always maternal guilt at every turn of the way. I drove home from depositing her at her Youth Training college with tears streaming down my face. The memories of our last few years together made our parting more sorrowful. I missed her a lot, and it was hard to get her on the phone at the stables where she worked. She loved working with horses and she settled well.

But just a few months after Rosie had left home, her own dad died from a heroin overdose. One of the worst memories of my life is of sitting at Rosie's workplace waiting to break the news to her. Her best friend and Dave were with me. Her boss went off to tell her she had visitors. When she saw us all gathered there, she knew something was seriously wrong. I realised instantly that she thought Craig had been killed so I broke the news to her straight away. Her first reaction was to feel sorry for her half-sister and brother who had lived with her dad. Then she cried briefly. She had been planning to visit him that winter. There had been a strong bond between them.

We went down to London together for the funeral. On the

way to the service, in the tube, she had a panic attack and wanted to turn back but I got her there. She showed little emotion and was pretty scathing about my tears. She assured me that she hadn't really felt that close to him and was perfectly all right.

She went back to work straight away, but after a few months, it became plain that the death was beginning to hit her. Her boss said she was breaking down in tears a lot and eventually she gave up the course and came home. This was an awful time. My grandmother and mother died within a few days of one another — two more funerals for us to attend all in the space of six months. We were numb with shock and grief. I watched over my daughter like a hawk. I knew she was under severe emotional pressure and she was exactly the same age as my own sister when the breakdown which led to her suicide had begun. Rosie spent weeks doing little but reading and watching TV. If I tried to talk to her about our losses, she snapped at me. And she would storm angrily out of the room if I started to cry with grief. Her friends had left school and the area, and Rosie was very isolated.

I was terrified that Rosie would lapse back into the horrendous problems of her early teens, but thankfully that awful scenario never came about. The period of rest seemed to work and after a few months she headed back to the city. A couple of years later, after loads of adventures and one or two misadventures, she went back to college to do an HND. As ever, I am on the lookout for problems, but she seems miraculously well-adjusted after all the upheaval. She makes friends easily, passed her driving-test first time, and is in much better shape than I was at her age. And she negotiates her relationships with men without my heavy compulsiveness. She has just passed the age at which my sister took her own life. Sometimes, there is still a tense edge between us but, on the whole, our relationship is good. Slowly we are moving towards friendship.

I have seen Rosie emerge from the vortex. And in the

family-album department of my brain, along with all the distress, are also stored the many magic moments — Rosie as a toddler, her winsome face framed by a mass of ringlets; her fairy dances at seven, bedecked in a spangled dress; Rosie as a young woman astride a mettlesome stallion jumping a towering hedge. These are the myriad occasions which somehow transcend the pain of being a mother.

Yet still I grieve that mothering, for me, has often been like the reopening of a grit-filled wound. Like Demeter in the ancient myth, I have had to travel, lamenting and alone, into the underworld to retrieve my lost daughter. In the legend, it is only when Persephone treads the earth again that winter loses its icy grip and the earth blossoms anew. This vital task of setting our daughters on the path of life, is, like Demeter's ordeal, often carried out in profound isolation. It is time some old legends were rewritten.

Appearance

Helena Hinn

There wasn't a moment when Kathy wasn't talking about appearance. Her appearance, her flaxen locks, her imagined fat tummy and the quasi-scientific measurement of various people's legs which invariably failed to come up to standard.

At twelve, her every value judgement was based on whether a person's looks were good or bad.

This obsession with looks was not her fault, for she acted as a siphon for the values of the society she was emerging into. Where young women are expected to channel all their energy into the narrow world of make-up, illusion and beguilement. As a distraction from politics, opinion, philosophy and real life.

Sovereignty

Frances Viner

In the eighties I was involved with a women's theatre company, The Raving Beauties. We used women's words to express women's experience, aspirations, power and pain. The impact of feminism was making its mark all right but for many, including myself, this outpouring seemed to indicate primarily one thing. I had constructed a life for myself which was out of sync with the new sense of self which was begging for expression. I found myself with a personal agenda which could not be accommodated by my relationship and domestic arrangements. This included my deep need to see myself as an artist – specifically a writer. For years I struggled to achieve this freedom – a struggle with its fair share of pain. But now, having lived as a single parent of two children for six years, I'm beginning to believe my destiny is to be happy and fulfilled after all. I recently produced my first play and realised I had exchanged trying to be happy for the state itself, the result of expression, choices, risk-taking and the co-operation of the universe; i.e. the result of things I had been told never to do – express, choose, take risks and believe in the co-operative beneficent universe.

And as I have been learning to live my life, my two children are learning to live theirs. We are growing up together and I think the main obligation we have to each other is to do just that – live. Don't mistake me. That includes hanging tough as well as hanging liberal. I have my limits and my kids often sharply remind me of them. As do the words of other mothers. 'They sleep, eat, lie on the sofa farting between bouts of abusing you, dope, themselves and listening to music which sounds like the last nail in your coffin.'

If we are looking for rocky terrain – the wilderness where my now happier spirit is tested – I'll admit it does exist. Alex, my gorgeous sixteen-year-old virgin daughter, is being offered the sex, drugs and rock and roll. In the past I have given her my trust and waited for her key to turn in the front door. When a friend, the mother of my daughter's best friend, said in passing, 'They lie about everything, don't they?' I was stunned. You could have fooled me. Quite.

Once I started looking for betrayal and deceit, inevitably they appeared, which opened up the deepest potential fracture in my relationship with my kids, the fact that they are half their father's. He had lied too – by default, preferring to omit the truth. It drove me barmy to think I was being lied to once again by someone I passionately loved.

As I watched my daughter grow to resemble her father I never felt a greater sense of foreboding than around this issue of 'truth'. Alex, I realised, did sometimes find it expedient to be promiscuous with the truth and this resonated with the worst abuse I had suffered in my partnership – chronic deceit. I talked to Alex about my need for a truthful response from her, which was not the same as wanting to own her inner life. Autonomy and truth can co-exist. But sometimes I felt as if I was just shouldering old burdens. Must I love him again in her?

The biggest self-deception in my family life had been that now my partner was not present under our roof he had also ejected out of the vehicle of fatherhood. He and it had crash landed somewhere and he was out there in no-man's land, waiting to get picked off by another woman. Although I wanted to be purged of my partner quick time, learn the lessons and move on, I have finally had to accept that for my children there can be no such projectile away from their dad. He's in the exchange of their cells — not the receding feature he has become in my new landscape — a High Sierra of independence, authenticity and poetry.

However, my daughter is not her father. Our rages and temperaments eventually return us to a plateau of love which he and I never discovered. The tests of love and patience which we regularly demand of each other seem designed to verify an everlasting bond. I suppose a relationship is like a new car — it has to be put through every imaginable test of endurance and safety in all possible conditions. Only then can it be said to work.

Truth, of course, is a double-edged sword and dealing with Alex's has been a mixed blessing. She already has a strong sense of her own identity which enables her to say what I would fear to utter. I still care too much about being liked. Her dispassionate, perceptive descriptions, often wickedly funny, dispatch the self-indulgent. Recently we were watching Cilla Black introduce star grandchildren who had engineered boggling secret delights for their grannies on *Surprise Surprise*. Alex commented that her grannie would be sitting at home 'biting through plates'. My kids sometimes find it difficult to remember they have a grannie and have to grovel their way back into her martyred affections when they miss the precious birthdays and other required tokens of affection.

At fourteen, Alex was thrown out of her all-girls school. I had no idea things were going so badly wrong. The wrong was in the eye of the beholders (teachers). I could not believe they were talking about *my daughter*. Education works best for individuals who fit the system, which has become increasingly lumbered with assessment rather than creativity and the celebration of uniqueness. I knew Alex as fun to be with and wonderfully alive, not a problem child bent on causing disruption. We found another school which seemed able to cope better with kids like Alex and she began to get some of the challenge and stimulation she needed. Although I have only spent a small amount of time teaching and even less talking to people in prison it strikes me that 'bad' and 'criminal' often chime with 'perceptive' and 'daring', but *not* 'middle-of-the-road'.

My struggle to acquire self-belief, the familiar subject of best-selling feminism, bred in me a passion for my daughter to avoid the 'I'm not worth it' cul de sac. I hope the consciousness-raising I have done is implicit in my attitude to her and all her works — most of the time. I read somewhere that children synthesise their parents, becoming greater than the sum of their parts. One and one make three. I observe there is a delicate relationship between the support and guidance I have to offer Alex and her emerging *different*, powerful authenticity. I do not even stand on the same path and I realise the new landscape she turns towards as she becomes a young woman is not a landscape I shall inhabit.

My son has only just entered the adolescent doldrums. He's thirteen and has recently started practising lying on the sofa for hours. Some of my main concerns for him and my relationship with him arise out of his parents' decision to part. Oscar repressed his pain and ate. Nearly six years on he's still overweight. The feelings of insecurity which Oscar experiences have made him more fearful and anguished than my daughter. I was relieved when he started to shout back and dare to be difficult.

All I want for my children is to see them light up with joy in life and enthusiasm for *something*. Ozzie lights up on stage. Dad again. And me. I had an earlier career on stage, but I came to see it as an attempt to deal with my feelings of profound unloveableness. I do not want my son to 'perform', driven by a need to prove to himself that he is adored and adorable. I am obliged to witness his explorations in the theatrical world while allowing the fears this brings forward about his damaged relationship with me and his dad. Have we loved our son enough for him to be free of crippling self-doubt? My intuition tells me yes, but I also know that some of the deep hurt Oscar experienced is still unexpressed and will probably have to wait for maturity to bring understanding of a past that cannot be changed, only accepted. The healing of deep wounds can take the inner work and forgiveness of more than one generation.

I remember the difficult relationship I had with my own mum. If only she had admitted to human weakness, doubt, error, difference, but her righteousness prevailed. Instead of learning to trust myself, especially my need to be an artist – a bohemian God forbid – I tried to please and protect Mother by appearing 'ordinary' and 'good'. It nearly killed me because I am extraordinary and bad. I lied so much to her and myself I forgot my truth. Although I profaned, fucked, took drugs, wasted, I did it shamefully, not playfully. However, I preferred self-sabotage to killing *her* with the sight of my unacceptable face.

Now with my own kids I want them to be themselves however uncomfortable it may be when they take risks and act without the fear that kept me frozen. If anything, I go to the other extreme and their untested views have too much sway. I exchange the traditional parochial supremacy of the older generation for awe at the beauty and raw talent of youth.

Parent and child defines a biological relationship not an absolute hierarchical one. Young people are destined to have more demanded of them than any previous generation if the planet is to meet the challenges with which it is currently struggling. We urgently need to love, listen to and respect them for what they must undertake, without being frightened that our status will be threatened as a result. The film *Kids*, considered shocking and exploitative by some, is not about kids. It's about our ailing society. Adults watching this movie are only shocked to the degree they have failed to know themselves and recognise their own turmoil. We cannot escape ourselves or our relationship with our young people. They are our future and they offer the most tender, fulsome arena in which to experience the loving unfettered power of self and others. Sovereignty.

Will I Survive?

Diane Gibson

I always thought boys would be easier to bring up — less moody than girls, no pre-menstrual tension, no worries about them getting pregnant, no period pains or keeping up with fashions. How wrong could I be? So far there's been acne and awkwardness, aggression, bad language, alcohol, drugs, and trainers that cost the earth — and their adolescence has only just begun.

I'm told adolescence is only a phase they go through, but I'd give a fortune to make it vanish. So far I've tried ignoring them, I've tried facing them head on armed with information and experience, I've tried putting myself in their shoes, I've tried to understand them, I've tried to communicate with them in their own language, I've tried blackmail, I've tried discipline, I have fought aggression with aggression, I've screamed and I've shouted and I've cried. I have tried every trick in the book. I have driven myself to despair. I have been to the edge of a nervous breakdown. I have taken anti-depressants. I am still no nearer to finding the solution. Maybe I have tried too hard.

I became a youth worker because I felt I could communicate with adolescents. My experience and empathy worked with them, but not with my own boys. I cannot cope with them. I feel guilty. I think terrible thoughts. I wish I had never given birth to them. I see them as monsters, as undesirables. I wish they were someone else's. Love feels like hate. I feel bitter and angry. I cry out, 'What have I done?' I wonder if my sons are just arseholes. I question whether they deserve me, their mother. I wish I were not their mother.

I feel like giving up. Let them go it alone. Let them ruin their lives, what do I care? But I do care. That's the problem. I care a lot. That's why I am struggling on. I look at other mothers. Their lives are better, simple, hassle-free. Their adolescent kids are not problems. So it must be me.

I look and feel as if I've been to hell and back. Will I survive? Will we survive?

To My Son

Pamela Lewis

My signal is not charted
on any navigational aid.

I am a small squat lighthouse,
built correctly and giving slightly
under an adolescent flurry.

I have stood here for some time
and am aware that my light
is often dim.

What homes on this poor beam
needn't bother; staying away
would be better.

It is a pity that sons
do not run away
to sea any more.

Taking It Hard

Colette O'Hare

The charge room was as bleak as ever, lino peeling, skirting boards scuffed by decades of dirty mops. Still, why bother; the punters at Cafe Rouge or Sofa So Good aren't likely to be much exercised by this unseen want of astheticism in their midst.

'We've been trying to ring you since 11 o'clock this evening.' The custody Sergeant began pleasantly enough. But he was lying, and as he said it he read it in my eyes. Sensing I was no novice, he dispensed with foreplay. 'Drunk and disorderly, criminal damage, resisting arrest, obstruction, breach of the peace . . .'

Liam leaned forward in his chair, elbows on knees, skinny neck and shaven head bent in sullen resignation.

A few days earlier he had been expelled from school. They wanted him to do English and Maths and PE. He wanted to be a rapper. When they spoke to him he answered in rap. When I spoke to him he looked out of the window. I told him he was letting people down. I told him that with his attitude he would never get anywhere. I told him . . . I told him . . . and then I thought . . . what *are* you talking about . . . what-the-fuck-are-you-talking-about? Listen to yourself . . . where did not letting people down ever get you?

He strode ahead of me down the empty High Street . . . tall, stick figure, arms and legs at crazy angles.

He went straight to his room. Seconds later the thud of the stereo through the ceiling . . . 'put on yo' shit kickers and kick some shit, put on yo' shit kickers and kick some shit . . .'

He'd be lying on his bed with his hands behind his head, a Fighting Irish baseball cap pulled over his eyes. Liam and his friends were a new breed; mixed race or second or third generation Brits. They are Irish because they choose to be – selective, it's true, but proud of the connection, in particular the association with intransigence and violence. The provocation that cannot fail. What being Irish meant was a Paddy's Night ruck down The Bush. They weren't particularly interested in Ireland. They owed it nothing. There were no apron strings. No slobbering sentimentality. No diddlie-aye music. Just that mocking, chilling contract. You made us. We are here. The ultimate Irish joke. The hybrid with unknowable potential, let loose.

He was the middle child, always a little separate, always slightly at odds with the world; but droll, laconic, with an early articulateness which would disguise cataclysmic learning difficulties to come. Maybe that's when the bad luck started. Or maybe it was all accidental. Maybe unwittingly I had assisted in the process – the non-standard name for a start. Can these things really be so arbitrary? The scowling two-year-old in the nursery sandpit yelling at an unsuspecting helper, 'No! No! My name isn't Leon! It's Liam! Liam! It's Irish! Don't you know anything?'

Or the 11-year-old addressing assembly on his last day at junior school. The Chlöes and Zöes and Jacks and Zacs preceding him had spoken of their hopes for the future – to feed the world, to save the rain forest. Liam stood centre stage. No visual aids, no show and tell, just one hand punching the air in clenched fist salute. 'I want Ireland to be free!' The camcorders held their breath. No applause for this one then, just stunned silence.

That touchiness, the importance of one's name in establishing one's identity, the contempt for the clumsy outsider ignorant of nuance – could such things really be inherited, can they really travel undiluted down the generations from North Belfast to West London?

After he had been expelled from school, I didn't see him for two days. Then I met him in Chiswick High Road. His right hand and forearm were in plaster. He'd been in a fight . . . that's all. Across the plaster was the Irish tricolour, meticulously drawn and coloured . . . green . . . white . . . gold. But the segments were disconnected, separate, fanned out like playing cards.

'Got any money?' he said.

'No.'

'Been shopping though, entcha?'

He grabbed the carrier bag, pawing at the contents. 'Size 16/18? Firm control? *Extra* large? Ra! Yo joke me na? Not *seriously* going to try to get into these are you, Mumsie? Dream on!'

A young, besuited, inoffensive-looking, red-haired man at the bus stop grinned, thinking to join in the fun.

Liam rounded on him, feinting a swing with the broken hand. 'Yo – ginger scum! Off our street!'

The man's head jerked back instinctively, his eyes dilating as the reinforced knuckle sandwich stopped inches short of his nose.

Liam weighed him up contemptuously. 'Look – they even got bigger umbrellas than the rest of us – so they can take up more fucking air and more fucking pavement and BE MORE FUCKING DRY!'

The young man stumbled onto a bus, twice tripping over the large, jauntily striped brolly which just minutes earlier must have seemed such a good idea.

'That wasn't funny, Liam,' I said.

He bared his shonkie teeth, tiny yellowed infant stumps. 'Oh, I don't know . . . it made me laugh.'

I persuaded him to go for an interview for an art foundation course. He insisted on taking a portfolio only of his graphic novel illustrations. He was interviewed by a fifty-something time server with an intricately clipped serial killer's beard. 'I see a lot of this kind of thing these days,' he sort of smiled, leafing through the drawings, 'most of it not quite as revolting as this though, I have to say.'

Outside Liam flung the portfolio to the ground, exploding into tears of fury. The pages blew all over the place. I picked up the empty folder and followed in silence.

He was offered a place on a YTS scheme. 'I ain't filling no fucking shelves at fucking Sainsbury's.' They put him in a graphic design studio where they thought his art work was well safe, so they did.

They offered him a job.

'And what did you say?'

'I told them I'd think about it.'

He lent his suit to his friend Steve for a court appearance. Well, creates a good impression, dinnit? Steve went down for four-and-a-half years, the suit went with him. He had to go to Steve's Mum's house in Brentford to get it back for the funeral . . . of his English grandmother. White shirt, narrow black tie, he looked good, like the lead in a Tarantino movie. He worked the room, then he said 'C'mon, let's get the fuck out of here.'

He would survive. He was learning the ropes, the hard way.

Possession

Julia Buxton

It was the end of another working day, and I was tidying my desk in a desultory manner; I was distracted and couldn't quite pinpoint why.

Of course, the obvious reason was worry about Lucy. My daughter, recently turned seventeen, had become a concern. She was supposed to be studying for A Levels at sixth-form college, but I doubted whether she attended very much. At about fifteen years old, she'd become a 'school refuser' — a polite word for truant. I'd drive her in in the mornings, she'd go to her form room for registration, then she'd disappear. I'd had many lengthy discussions with her class teacher, her headmistress, the Educational Welfare Officer and the child psychologist, but no amount of persuasion, bargaining, bribery or threatening would induce her to attend.

We'd therefore moved her from school because we assumed she was unhappy. She'd never actually expressed an opinion; she simply didn't want to be there and had voted with her feet.

But I suspected that nothing much had changed and that she merely went to college in the morning as a gesture to keep her out of trouble with me. Then I imagine she left, and did whatever it was she did for the rest of the day.

On this particular afternoon, she was genuinely on holiday from college. I'd suggested that she come and join me for lunch, and perhaps we'd do some shopping. (Although she was often surly and recalcitrant, I still loved her dearly and enjoyed her company whenever I could get it.) She hadn't turned up. I'd rung home, she wasn't there. Annie, my assistant, knew me well enough to realise I was anxious, however hard I tried to disguise it. 'She'll have forgotten,' she tried to reassure me. 'Never!' I countered. 'A free lunch and the possibility of some clothes or make-up? She wouldn't miss that! She wanted to come.'

'Well, perhaps she had to go elsewhere. You know how unreliable she is about her movements.'

I knew, logically, that Annie was right, but something made me uneasy.

At about five to six, the telephone rang. Annie answered it. Struggling into my coat, I waved my hand and shook my head as if to say, 'I'm not here'. Annie nodded, smiling.

She spoke for a moment or two. Then I heard her say, 'Who is this, please?'

Her voice, normally light and cheerful, had altered subtly; it conveyed concern. I turned and saw she was frowning. Her face seemed to have paled.

'Who is it?'

She covered the mouthpiece with her hand. 'It's a man. He won't say who he is. All he'll tell me is that it concerns Lucy.'

I almost wrenched the handset from her as she held it towards me.

'This is Julia Buxton, Lucy's mother. Who is this?' I thought that there must have been some sort of accident or — bizarre idea — that she'd been abducted. When the man told me he was a police sergeant, I gasped and sank into a chair. Annie ran around her desk. 'What's happened? What's happened?'

'Why are you phoning me? Is my daughter all right?' (Please, please God, let him tell me nothing's happened to her.)

'She's not ill or injured, if that's what you mean.'

'She's not – dead?'

I thought – unbelievably – that he almost laughed, but I was in no state to challenge him.

'No, she's not dead, but whether you think she's all right is a different matter.'

I was beginning to get frantic – I felt he was playing games.

'What then?'

'She's been arrested.'

'Arrested?' Now Annie gasped. 'On what charge?'

The thought of shop-lifting crossed my mind; inexcusable but perhaps possible to explain as a childish prank by an unhappy adolescent. But it wasn't that at all; it was worse, much worse.

'Possession of drugs, madam. I think she'd like to see you. She is, after all, a minor. She's at Manor Road Police Station.'

'Drugs? What drugs?'

I imagined marijuana, but had thought the police were more lenient these days – I'd heard they usually had a stern word with youngsters and then let them off. Perhaps she'd had some pills on her. I knew she'd taken Ecstasy at raves – her bravado was such that she'd boasted to me about it, and I'd certainly not approved. But, wishy-washy liberal of a parent that I was, I'd kept my mouth shut.

I was utterly unprepared for his next word, so much so that I thought he was using the feminine version of 'hero', and couldn't imagine who he was referring to. Me? Her? Then the light dawned.

Involuntarily, I said, 'Heroin? Oh, no!'

I was shocked and dazed, and poor Annie stood by, not completely understanding but able to guess enough to realise, and not knowing quite what to do for the best. I knew, however, that whatever she'd done I just wanted to be with Lucy.

'Where is she? I'm coming now. Where will I find her?'

I couldn't believe what he said next, didn't imagine these things happened.

'She's safe enough. She's in a cell.'

What? Locked up? I was utterly horrified; that anyone could do that to a seventeen-year-old girl, and that a seventeen-year-old girl could do something worthy of this treatment.

'She's in a cell,' he repeated. 'And cells are locked.'

I put the telephone down in total disbelief. Annie said, 'Are you okay? Can I do anything? Shall I come with you?'

I shook my head. Then a thought struck me. 'Just do one thing for me, Annie, please.'

'Anything.'

'Don't tell anyone. Just don't tell anyone. I'm so ashamed.' I finally burst into tears. 'I must be a terrible mother.'

Annie tried to reassure me, crouching next to me, stroking my face, cuddling me as I sobbed for several minutes. Eventually I managed to speak. I thanked her and said, as confidently as I could manage, 'Just go home, Annie. I'll be all right. I'll see you tomorrow.'

When I got to the police station, Lucy was tearful but defiant. She was allowed home on bail 'on her own recognisance' – that is, no money was required. She had to return in a month to get the result of the arrest. We were told it was likely to be a caution, but were reminded that heroin is a Class A drug. I prayed she wouldn't wind up in court, and was honest enough to realise that I feared for my own reputation as well as her future. I felt a miserable failure.

On the way home she was not very forthcoming, but I tried to make her appreciate how very upset and concerned I was. I said a lot of 'How could you?' and 'Whatever possessed you?' and 'Are you mad?' At one point she said, 'It's my life. It's shitty.' I couldn't grasp whether she meant it was her life and she'd do as she pleased, or her life was shitty so she did drugs. I didn't press; I was as confused as she seemed to be, probably more so.

But she seemed quite unable or unwilling to say sorry. We didn't say much more on the journey, which was probably just as well. When we got to the house, she said, quite quietly, that she was going to her room. I said okay, but that we had to talk later. I then went and poured myself a large drink. The fact that alcohol and drugs both blur the edges and, in excess, neither one is better than the other, did not escape me. But I needed that drink. If I had never had my very first drink, I thought, I wouldn't need this one. Perhaps there was a lesson there to be learnt in respect of Lucy.

The result of Lucy's arrest was that she was cautioned. She was suitably contrite, apparently genuinely. The inspector was kindly but uncompromising. He explained very carefully how a conviction could affect her life forever, let alone the devastating effects of the drug itself.

In a way this episode was a relief. Lucy's behaviour had been so ghastly; now I knew why. At least I had something to come to terms with, to comprehend. However devastating the facts, they are always easier to handle than uncertainty – I only cry when I don't understand.

But that was by no means the end of the matter. If I thought the fear of further arrest and a criminal record had cured her, then I had bargained without the appeal of the drug. For a while I lulled myself into a false sense of security, forcing myself to believe that any sensible person would have been shocked into recognising that the heroin trail was destined to end in disaster. I realise now that I deluded myself by putting certain clues down to teenage moodiness and rebellion, and subconsciously refusing to accept others that were inexplicable. Lots of little things, in isolation, could perhaps be ignored but, put together, meant only one thing. She was still using. I remember one night, in the early hours, waking, absolutely rigid, eyes wide open and seeing, in the darkness, facts flying together and fitting like a jigsaw. There was the coated tongue, the suddenly spotty skin, the constipation, the occasional nausea. Her reluctance to see her formerly closest friends, a favourite aunt, her father. There was the incense, the candles. The rapidly diminishing roll of kitchen foil. Her constant demands/entreaties for more money, odd things going missing, often from my purse. And so on . . . It was circumstantial only – you couldn't convict anyone on this evidence – but I had to acknowledge I would be a fool to disregard what I knew I saw.

Lucy had none of the attributes you hope to associate with the young; she wasn't healthy or energetic, she certainly wasn't carefree. She carried a burden of guilt which surrounded her like a cloud. But she wouldn't talk – at least not to me. We lived an artificial existence, both in the same house, me often upset and pleading, though I tried to be resolute, and supportive if she appeared to need it. She skulked around the place, avoiding me; she stayed out late and sometimes didn't come in at all. Every single thing I had ever tried to teach her about respect and responsibility and reliability went out of the window. I grew to be unsurprised, but I never got used to it. She had become a stranger.

Rightly or wrongly, I tried to manage the whole business myself, without involving her father. This was partly because of my own sense of failure – I didn't want to give him ammunition for criticism – and partly because I didn't want him to hate her. The relationship between him and me had been strained but civilised; he adored Lucy and she him, but I wasn't sure his affection could tolerate this shock, and I knew she needed him.

Other things happened, devastating things, like my discovery that she'd pawned ('but it wasn't stealing – I was going to get them back') all my little Victorian rings, love tokens from my two grandfathers and a great-grandfather to their fiancées, to feed her habit. The £200 I paid out to retrieve these items was just one of the many financial prices her addiction cost me.

One aspect of the addiction which both disgusted and

scared me was that I discovered addicts burn holes in everything — furniture, carpets, clothes, bed linen. They smoke cigarettes heavily and, when they're dozy from the drugs, they drop the cigarettes. Burn holes are a feature of a heroin addict's habitat. They also light lots of candles — to disguise smells? I lived daily — or nightly — in fear of fire.

One day, whilst I was snooping (an inexcusable but irresistible urge when broken promises and suspicion are driving you insane), I found blank cheques in Lucy's bedroom, quite obviously stolen from a friend of mine who asked her to babysit from time to time. My friend's son adored her. I went cold as I tried to imagine whether other things from my friend's house might have been taken. But I couldn't think of a way to safeguard her home without actually telling her, so I stayed silent. However, next time she asked Lucy to babysit, I stalled and didn't pass the message on. I knew it was only a temporary solution, but couldn't think what else to do. With every new crisis or problem that occurred, the long term looked bleaker. I became able only to deal in short-term decisions. It was hell.

I tried bargaining with Lucy, hoping for good behaviour in return. For example, I told her that, if she wanted my continuing support, she had to agree to attend a Chemical Dependency Clinic with me. I almost didn't expect her to turn up for the appointment; she'd promised, but promises meant very little these days. But she came. She was withdrawn and resentful; we drove up together in an uncomfortable silence. Then, when we got there, she sat with the counsellor, anger radiating from her tense body, and refused to say anything. I suddenly realised what she was up to. She'd promised to come, but she hadn't promised to say anything. The session was not a success.

It was without doubt the most miserable period of my life. I had thought my separation from my husband had been tough, but it was never life-threatening. With Lucy, I lived each day in the expectation that the police would contact me again to say she'd overdosed, or that she had been arrested for dealing, or stealing, or soliciting. It was a knife-edge existence and I never relaxed.

I tried to be honest with my feelings, but I am not a very instinctive person. I was brought up to control my emotions, and also always to see the other person's point of view. Therefore I had a tendency, throughout this ordeal, constantly to consider Lucy's pain rather than my own, and to feel inadequate and guilty. I tried not to say 'why me?', because I knew these things happened to people with no rational explanation. I suppressed my true emotions until, one day, someone in whom I'd confided said, 'How do you really feel?' I realised then how very angry I was. It did me a great deal of good to acknowledge that I was furious with this child. I had done everything I could to make her feel secure and loved, given her opportunities, praised her even when she didn't deserve it, and nurtured her carefully, sometimes to my own detriment. How could she do this to me? I didn't feed on this anger, but I stored it away, allowing that it was there. The knowledge did me good.

Most of this time was horrible. But they say that which does not kill you makes you strong. There were lessons to be learnt for both of us. I began writing as a sort of catharsis – this piece is one result of that. I also thought more about my life, its juxtaposition with others, and I believe I began to grow. I learned to accept, as it says in the Serenity Prayer, the things I could not change. Whether I also had the courage to change the things I could change, and the wisdom to know the difference – well, I'm still working on those.

Then one day Lucy announced she'd found a counsellor, and had enrolled in a detox scheme. Suddenly it seemed the sun might come out again. Now we stumble on, hoping that this will resolve the problem in future, but by no means sure. I experience days of hope and days of despair, but try to keep the worst times from her, though it does her no harm to know how I feel, to know what she's doing to me. I joined a support group and discovered that there are many, many ordinary parents out there who've brought up their offspring to the best of their ability, only to find themselves now confused and shocked at the route their child has taken. How sick they get of other parents saying, 'Sarah's in her second year of university now; and how is so-and-so getting on?' They're left with no response except to lie or be evasive, and it's all very depressing. And disappointing. One had such hopes, such aspirations, and they're now all turned to dust, or so it seems.

I have evolved certain theories about people and drugs – circumstances have forced me to become an amateur expert. One is that these days, almost everyone comes into contact with drugs and has the opportunity to try them. There are those who are never tempted, and those who try and soon reject the experience as not for them. Then there are those who develop a habit and therefore a problem. For some, it is a temporary phase which may last several years, but which they eventually overcome. For others, it is a life sentence. I am praying and hoping that Lucy's experience falls into the third category.

I have also come to the conclusion that some people seem not to have enough natural uplifting hormones to cope with the down side of life – which can, after all, be pretty awful. When it comes to dulling the pain, we have access to a variety of means: alcohol, religion, counselling, prescribed drugs. Are they so very different from illegal drugs?

I've had the odd revealing insight into the appeal of heroin. A recovering addict whom I met through a friend explained that heroin was 'like a love affair. If I'd been offered an attractive woman companion for the night, or a fix, I'd have taken the gear anytime. It's a seduction, the most delightful experience you can imagine.' And we *can* only imagine; we daren't try, not even in an effort to understand our loved one. But we see the misery it creates in its wake, the craving, the physical pain and the mental anguish. Who can tell why anyone, knowing what we all know, commences that journey destined almost certainly for disaster? Lucy never explained it to me. Perhaps she revealed it only to her counsellor; perhaps she never truly understood it herself. It was almost certainly an attempt to escape, and may have related to the loss of her father as a presence in the house. Who knows? But others endure this experience and don't turn to heroin. Maybe it was as simple as a flaw in her personality, a need which was temporarily filled by this pain-killing drug. But it's a deceiver, this drug; it replaces one pain with another far greater agony, one that possesses the whole family, one that every member has to endure.

I've stopped making suggestions to Lucy – I believe that she must now motivate herself. She's in her early twenties now. I was married with a baby by her age. That doesn't mean I think she should do the same, but I know she is capable of taking personal responsibility. And she is starting to do so. She has suggested, unprompted by me, that she might check into a residential rehab scheme. Hallelujah! She'd be out of my hair for a while (I'm being honest with my emotions again – and that's good for me). No more checking my purse, no more anxious nights wondering if/when she would come in. Let's hope she does it – I won't push, but my fingers are crossed.

I think Lucy's learning to have faith in me again, to trust my motives. Maybe she thought I drove her father out, thus betraying her. She doesn't seem so bitter now – and she is starting to communicate with me. She also talks to her father in a much more relaxed way, though not completely openly – she's not had the confidence to tell him her secret. I did though – I needed his support. The problem was more than I could bear alone. And, guess what, he doesn't hate her – how stupid of me ever to imagine that he could!

How long it will take me to trust her again is a different question – she has a lot to prove. But she is still my daughter. Any mother will understand that, after the investment of nine months' pregnancy and many years' nurturing, it's hard to let go. But let go I must; I have to allow her to make her own decisions, good or bad. I cannot go through it for her, I cannot change her; all I can do is love her.

This Power

Emma Marx

Most
she resents
you,
her son,
forbidding
her own home
peace.

Against All Odds

Liz Morgan

My beautiful son died last year and I am heartbroken. Had he lived another 6 weeks he would have been 21. As it was, his friends celebrated for him. Never first at anything in life, perhaps in a perverse way, being first in death might have appeased him.

Darren was never an easy child, but at the age of 12 or 13 things became markedly worse. We decided to try a weekly boarding school for him and every Sunday afternoon, when the time came to return to school, he would withdraw into a corner, turn deathly white, and need to be persuaded into the car. Often he ran back into the house on the pretext of looking for something. When he finally waved goodbye, he left us feeling almost as unhappy as he was. We persuaded him to go for the first term because we felt that this school offered great opportunities for him in the future. We know he was homesick but hoped he would be happier when he made some friends there. Afterwards we found out that he was being badly bullied by the children and by some of the staff. One of the masters was very strict, punishing him for small misdemeanours like talking in class by making him stand to attention for hours on end in dark corners of the school or even outside, alone at night. Suspicions that this man abused some pupils have since arisen.

My son began to sniff glue and was suspended for three weeks. When he returned to school, life became even more difficult and after a short time we were asked to remove him.

There followed a period of several months without school of any kind and although Darren was relieved to be at home again he was well aware that he was fast becoming a misfit. The glue-sniffing became worse. Once, after searching the house for him, my daughter and I found him unconscious on his bedroom floor. He was lying half-under the bed and it was hard to see him. Another time we had to force our way into the bathroom, to find him slumped behind the door. We had to shout his name, shake him, and make him drink black coffee in order to rouse him. Then, when it seemed safe to let him sleep for a few hours, we steered him back to bed. Sometimes, in less extreme cases, he would simply become incoherent, talking too fast, laughing inanely, and boasting of skills he did not possess. As the effects wore off he would become a little boy again needing reassurance and cuddles.

The following term he joined the local school and was placed in the top class. He did well for a few weeks until his poor writing skills began to let him down, and once more he fell behind the others. Orally he was brilliant. He was desperate to make friends and would join in any plans and activities. Because of his high intelligence, he would elaborate on them, go further than they could. But this applied to negative pastimes as well as positive. If others were playing truant locally, he would go one better and show them how to travel to Leeds or London. He was getting into trouble again. I became very worried about him and decided to enlist the help of Social Services.

But far from improving the situation, this made matters decidedly worse. Educational psychologists, social workers and even psychiatrists arranged meetings with the family and delved and probed into our affairs, looking for some dark secret which did not exist. Darren became self-conscious and embarrassed and his behaviour rapidly deteriorated. He refused school completely and soon I found out that he had begun to to take drugs. He was removed to an Assessment Centre but he continually ran away, arriving back at our door at all hours of the day or night. Against orders I fed him and calmed him down before driving him back myself, instead of allowing the police to come and take him away. We still loved him and he wanted to be with us, but we had to give the Assessment Centre a chance to change him. Needless to say, they found him almost as difficult to handle as we did and were no more successful in getting him to attend school.

At the end of a year, Darren came home again, and we were all delighted. But he found it harder than ever to become integrated into local life. He took refuge in sleeping all day and he stayed awake all night, the noise of his TV or music ensuring that I didn't sleep either. The situation was a nightmare for him and for me.

The more involved the professionals became the more difficult Darren was, and the more drugs he wanted. The only way to acquire drugs was to buy them, and the only place to get money was from me. All the bullying he had endured in the past was now directed towards me, until I parted with money. His favourite trick was to trap me in a room with him. He would stand with his back to the closed door, dangling the house keys from his long fingers and talk and talk and talk, explaining why he *needed* my money. I would start out calmly determined not to give in to his threats, but as the time passed and I realised that I could not break him, *I* became desperate and *he* became excited until it was obvious that he would snap and break something, which he did. Sometimes a window, sometimes a favourite ornament.

Often, sensing trouble ahead, I would leave the house and slip away quietly. I couldn't risk the noise of the car's engine in case he realised I was leaving. If he did, he would follow me. As his demands became greater and more frequent I appealed to the professionals for help but without much success. They had no idea how to stop what was happening and as he grew older they began to lose interest.

Despite the dreadful effect on my life, my one aim was to free Darren from drugs and gradually discover the lovely intelligent boy that I knew was still there somewhere. But try as I might, I could not succeed and finally the situation became so bad that we agreed to part company. We both wept at the parting and declared our love for each other.

Over the next few years, I lived for the occasional ringing of the phone, always sensing when a call was coming, and staying indoors ready for it. They would arrive from some city to tell me his news, sometimes good, usually bad. He always gave me his address as he moved from one sordid bedsit to another, making sure that he didn't disappear into obscurity. He always told me when 'friends' stole his money or belongings. Once he rang to say he had a new flat and had decorated it himself. He was so proud, that time. Sometimes he was distraught and I calmed him, talking for as long as he needed to, always feeling better for the contact. Finally he began to talk of hospitals and doctors, shaking his pills against the phone so that I could hear how many he had. But when I suggested visiting him, it was never convenient.

A short time later I had a call from a stranger, a friend of Darren's. He told me that Darren was dying of leukaemia. I did go to him then. He had found real friends at last and was staying with them. His face lit up with pleasure when he saw me and I hid my tears as I hugged him. His last words were 'I love you, Mam.'

I miss him so much. Life is empty without him. I glimpse him in the streets, on the underground, on the buses. I just wish that some day he would come home again.

An Interview

Meg Graham

I've got to the stage now that whatever anyone wants to do, if they want to point the finger, if they want to blame me, then that's fair enough. Blame me. Go on, blame me. It doesn't matter anymore.

He's never been an easy child. He's always been quite stubborn and had his own ideas about things and we clashed quite a few times. But we were always terribly close, really, really close, and it was good. Craig was closer to me than my husband ever was. But he saw a lot of things he shouldn't have seen and heard a lot of things he shouldn't have heard when he was wee. He saw me being abused by Colin. He heard me being abused. He heard me being raped. Afterwards he used to come up and cuddle me and say, 'Never mind, Mum.' God, that was when he was only four and five. He shouldn't have had to act like that. He shouldn't have had to worry about whether his mum was all right. That's part of his problem, but it's only part of it.

I think Craig would have been the way he is regardless of the sort of background he had, regardless of his upbringing.

Anyway we muddled along for quite a long time. We struggled through till Craig was five years old. Then I left. There was no bravery in it. It was total fear. I didn't know where to go or I'd have left years before. In the end I went to the Citizen's Advice. A nice woman talked to me and I sat and admired the tattoos on her arm. I said, 'I want to leave my husband and I don't know where to go', and she said, 'It's dead simple. It's no problem. You go to Women's Aid. Does he batter you?' and I said, 'Oh no, no, no, he doesn't batter me. I'm not a battered wife.' Because I was ashamed. You see, to begin with I really loved this guy. I had this idea in my head that all he needed was some stability in his life, all he needed was someone to love him enough, to understand him. What cracks me up now is that I *knew* he was violent.

Craig was always difficult. Always hard work. But things changed the night I went out. He should have stayed with the babysitter but he wanted to stay with two older boys at the end of the street. Anyway Craig went on and on and on, and in the end I gave in. I gave in to him and I'll never forgive myself for it. I left him with the option if he wasn't happy to come back home. I had no real concerns because one of the laddies had babysat for me. And I came back at two in the morning and my son was running up and down the middle of the street, hysterical, screaming. A nine-year-old! And I'm trying to make sense of it, trying to make sense of what's he's saying. He's hurling abuse at everything and everybody. He wouldn't come in the house and I spent about an hour in this cul-de-sac trying to calm my hysterical son. In the end I went into the house and left the door open. About half-an-hour later he came in, snuck up to bed and fell asleep. Over that weekend, he was acting really bizarre, going out and climbing back in the window. He wouldn't let me bath him. He smelled of perfume. His eyes were bloodshot. These bits and pieces came together and I phoned the doctor. He came out, and Craig was taken into hospital where they checked him over because I was scared he'd been abused in some way. They said penetrative sex had not taken place, but I'm sure he had been abused in some way. We'll never know. I'll never get to the bottom of it. That's when everything started for Craig. That's when it all went wrong. After that it went from bad to worse. Every day. Every day there was something. He was attacking neighbours. He was breaking windows. He was being abusive towards me and towards the other two children. For a few months he was a different boy and then things settled down and he was okay. And I thought, Thank God for that. We seem to have got through it.

But it hadn't gone away. It had only gone deeper. And somehow, somewhere along the line, everything was sparked off again. He started being really terrible at school, shouting and screaming. And what really concerned me was that every time he opened his mouth it was a sexual thing he'd come out with. I remember noting that everything he said had something to do with some sexual act. At school, every day something happened. He was spitting on other children. He was attacking other children for no reason. And the school were looking to me, and pointing the finger at me, and asking me about my home life, and I was pissed off with people pointing the finger at me because I was trying desperately to help Craig. He found it so difficult to talk to me about it, and he wouldn't talk to anyone else at all. He wouldn't talk to the social workers. He says he's told me what he knows which isn't very much. Whether he knows more, I don't know. I don't know. I think Craig blames me for not doing more. Oh God, I wanted to murder the boys he stayed with that night, I wanted to set their house on fire. I wanted to call Colin because I thought that would kill two birds with one stone because he'd get done for murder and then he'd get put in jail. But most of all I wanted to murder those two guys. I wanted them to have some of the pain they were causing me and my family. The other side of me knew that wasn't the answer. They were probably victims as well. They must have their own problems. But God did I hate them for a long long time.

In the end Craig was beyond everyone's control. I couldn't have anyone in the house because he was absolutely over the top, jumping on the settee, and shouting and swearing, and climbing in and out of the windows. My friend Aden tried to speak to him and say, 'Look at the effect you're having on your mum and look at what you're doing to yourself' and that night ended up even worse because my son said he was going to stab Aden, and Aden said something along the lines of, 'Well, go on then,' so Craig went into the kitchen and brought through two big carving knives and would have stabbed Aden had we not, between us, restrained him. You could tell by his eyes. He would have. The school grilled me over and over again about my home life. I'm sure they thought I was doing something to Craig. I was upset enough about what was happening to Craig without people suspecting me. The school suggested I went to Social Work. I went up and down to Social Work, two or three times a week. The social workers did the same. They grilled me over and over. And then things seemed to settle down again for a bit because that's when I met David. They did settle down. I kept my relationship with David separate from the house. He'd only seen the kids a couple of times. He wasn't involved with the kids at all because I was thinking I have to keep these two things separate. In order to survive. And because I needed something for myself. I told David nothing about the problems I was having with Craig.

But it didn't work out. It didn't. School began to get the worst of it and again they were looking to me for the answer, and I didn't have an answer. I hated being scrutinised as a person and a parent. I don't like that at all. I'm very uncomfortable with it. I was sick to death with the hassle and people coming to the door, and the school ringing all the time. I was up at school all the time. Up at Social Work because school recommended it. They all seemed to be more interested in me than Craig. They were looking for the obvious, and I wasn't prepared to buy the obvious. That I was a single parent, bringing up three children on my own. What did I expect! That Craig was from an abusive relationship. What did I expect! They were all looking for convenient labels to put on us but the labels never fitted very well, and over the years I've had to take the labels away altogether. At that time, I began to think I must have contributed. I must have. But I don't quite view it that way anymore. I'm not so hard on myself.

Things got just so bad. By the time he was thirteen I dreaded him coming in. One night I gave him my last fifty pence just to get him out of the bloody door. I would give him anything just to get him away from me because he would follow me round the house, criticising me, over and over and over. 'This is crap for tea.' 'What are you doing that for?' 'Why haven't I got a clean jumper?' and it was constant, constant, constant all the time. He would wait outside the toilet door until I came out, and while I was in there he'd be mouthing on and on. Until I just couldn't stand him being in the house. And because he was having problems at school he was getting excluded so what happens? He's with me twenty-four hours a day. And I was working at the time as well. Trying to. Only every time the school phoned me up they expected me to drop what I was doing and go running to sort out Craig, which I had to do. I was getting worn out. I couldn't sleep. I had a sound track running, 'Have to get sorted out! What am I doing wrong? What am I doing wrong? Better look at myself. See what's going on. It's not good enough. I must try harder. Try harder.' It was like trying to apply yourself one hundred per cent, one hundred per cent of the time. And I'm still trying to pretend to David that everything is hunky-dory. I'm thinking, God, I really like that guy, I'm really attracted to him. We think the same, we can communicate, God I don't want him to find out about Craig because he's the only thing in my life, the only thing that's just for me. And if I lose this . . .

It got really crazy. I remember sitting on the bus with Craig. You had to be ready for action. Always. Sitting on the bus was a nightmare because he'd start swearing and giving people dirty looks. Then you'd get up to get off the bus and you're trying to stay calm and you've got all these women, yes women, tutting and saying, 'She can't control her child'. And I'm saying, 'Come on Craig, calm down, and we'll see about this when we get home' and he's going, 'Fucking! Fucking! Fucking!' and everybody's looking at you, and we're getting up to get off the bus and he just takes this wee guy by the scruff of the neck. He hadn't even looked at him but Craig started battering hell out of him. And I'm trying to get off the bus and my son's battering this laddie! And I've got hold of my son, and he's got this laddie! And I'm dragging him off, and I've got him off, and of course everybody in the bus is talking about me and talking about him. How can I hack this?

In the end, when I was working, the phone calls from school were coming on a daily basis. And it wasn't for minor things. He was shouting and swearing at the teachers. He was flying at children in the playground who weren't even looking at him. He was attacking children. He was running round the school like a mad thing. At that point he had transferred his anger from me and was taking it out on other people. In the house, me and him, we were fine. But the school couldn't control him. They'd phone up and say, 'You've got to come and collect him again.' I'd go to collect him and say, 'I'm sorry' for the hundredth time and burst into tears. I'd take him home and calm him down and try to get to the bottom of it. But there never was an explanation. He didn't have an explanation. Later, he'd be out playing and the same night I'd get someone coming to my door saying, 'Your son is picking on my child' or 'Your son has thrown a shopping trolly at me' or 'Your son has smashed my window' or 'Your son has thrown a football at my child's head'. It was like there was no way of escaping. Everywhere I went, I was living Craig's life. I went to work; I had to leave because of Craig. I'm at home; somebody comes to the door because of Craig. Everything was ruled by Craig. And it drove me crazy. It cracked me up. Until it got to the stage that I couldn't stand him being in the house with me. Again I was up at Social Work. Regularly. Once a week. Twice a week. It ended up with us there for days on end. By then I couldn't talk any more. I was crying all the time.

And I'd started a relationship with this really brilliant guy so of course Craig stepped up another gear. I thought, 'I'm going to have to come clean with this guy. I'm going to have to tell him. And if I were him, I'd run a mile.' I didn't know what to tell him because I didn't want to lose that relationship. I really really didnae. I thought a lot of the guy. I thought this could be good. Anyway, I phoned him up one night and I just cried. By that point, I was crying all the time. He came across straightaway and I spilled the whole lot out. He said, 'The two of us are going to Social Work tomorrow morning and we're going to talk this over.' Well we went, and they grilled us. We went there for three days on the trot, three consecutive days from half past nine until half past three, and umpteen different social workers came in to talk to us, and I had to relay my story over and over and over again. Until on the third day, David had to physically help me walk up to the Social Work department. Still they grilled *me* about *my* life, about *my* character, about *my* relationship with David. It was horrendous. They made it worse. I got to the stage where I couldn't talk any more. I could not speak. And I shook from head to toe. They came in at one point and said they were concerned for my mental health and they wanted a doctor to see me.

David and a male social worker took me along to the surgery. It was packed; I couldn't even walk in the door. I was shaking like a leaf, I hadn't slept for days, I'd been worried sick, I was crying all the time, and I was hiding under David's jacket and holding on to him for grim death. And I found I could not hear half the time. It was like I was going to black out. And I couldn't understand what people were saying. Things were moving too fast. And I couldn't talk any longer. I could not speak. So they took me along in that state and sat me in front of the doctor. I hid my face and I rocked backwards and forwards on the chair and I was shaking and crying. The guy must have thought, 'There's one together mother there!' First he gave the social worker a grilling for bringing me in in such a state. He said he should have been called out to see me. Then he said he'd never seen me before in my life, and for all he knew, I was always like this, and he couldn't tell them what was wrong. That was good! Then he gave me a prescription for two types of valium, and suggested a community psychiatric nurse. By then I'd given up trying to tell people the problem was Craig, not me. I *was* a problem by that stage. But I wasn't a problem when I had been up every week saying, 'I can't cope with Craig. Craig's driving me nuts. He's attacked me. He's attacked one of the other children.' Nobody would bloody well take that on.

We left the surgery and they bundled me into a taxi. I crouched on the floor behind the driver's seat with my head covered. I remember the social worker asked me if I was all right! Of course I was all right. I was curled up in a ball on the floor in the back of the cab. I was fine! I was great! Just brilliant!

David said he would look after me with the help of a psychiatric nurse who came the next day. I know he was nice, and I know he told me my coping mechanism was overloaded and had broken down. He told me Craig would be taken into care and the other two would be looked after. I don't know what he looked like because I wouldn't look at anybody then. Only David. I kept my hands firmly clasped over my face. After maybe an hour of David sitting with me and being ever so tolerant, ever so calm, ever so reassuring, I would put my hands down and talk and function and think again.

A couple of days later Craig went missing. None of the social workers on duty had seen Craig so they couldn't pick him up because they didn't know what he looked like. So one social worker took me in her car, and another social worker took David in his. Even then, they kept grilling us until we were exhausted. If you'd asked me anything that day, I'd have answered. It was like a prison camp interrogation. I would have answered anything to anybody. In the end it was David who spotted Craig. And although they told me afterwards that everything had gone fine, of course it hadn't. David had had to sit on him in the middle of the road to stop him running off, a crowd had gathered, and the police had come along. Craig was finally bundled into a car and taken to a Family Resource Centre where he ripped all the posters off the wall and punched holes in the place. David was brilliant. He talked to Craig, promised to return the next day, explained that I was in no state to look after him.

I can't remember much about that time. But I remember my birthday. Birthdays in our house were always in the morning and the kids would come running through with some sort of present, usually stuff they'd made themselves because they knew I liked that. This was a birthday, but I was in a flat and it wasn't my flat. It wasn't even David's flat. It was shared accommodation. One of my kids was in care and the other two were being looked after by somebody else. I was worth nothing. I wasn't worth a shit. So I decided I would just keep on taking tablets until I blacked out because I didn't want a birthday. I didn't let anyone buy me a card. Or if they did I ripped them up. I didn't want that birthday because birthdays included my children so I popped pills. When David wasn't looking I was popping pills. He didn't see me do it, but he saw me get worse and worse as the evening went on. More drowsy. More dopey. That was when he said, 'If you're not able to be responsible, I won't be able to look after you. You'll have to go into hospital.' That shocked me into behaving. For a while.

It was a long time before I could go home. But gradually I went back. For short periods, then longer. I was panicky. First I went to the front door on my own. Then down the road on my own. Then to the shops on my own. Going on the bus alone was a great big one. I kept in contact with the kids on the phone. I spoke to them often. Craig said I sounded funny. It must have been the drugs. They found a foster parent for him. The social worker took me along to meet her, because I couldn't go anywhere by myself. They took me to this woman's house, and I'm sitting there drinking tea out of her best china, and I didn't even contribute because I couldn't take anything in. But I saw Craig and Craig saw me. I did see my son.

I was back at work when I took the next big downer. I had stayed late after work with a friend who was leaving – because my three kids were in care so I didn't have to hurry home to them. It was nice because we had a bottle of wine and a good laugh. We got a taxi back and she got off at her house, and I got off at mine. I walked in and there were no lights on. There was nobody there. My children weren't there. I always felt guilty if ever I felt happy, or found myself laughing. I thought, 'Oh for goodness sake! What have you got to laugh about? Your three kids are in care.' So I started eating pills. Then I panicked in case I had not done it properly and would end up a vegetable so I worked my way through the medicine cabinet. I phoned the Samaritans. I told them I didn't see much point in living. I told them my whole life was such a bloody mess. They said nothing to make me feel hopeful. Then I phoned a women's group and told them what I'd done. So the next thing was the ambulance men coming through the front door. I was really laid back. Like I was dreaming. Oh, I was wishing I would pass out, I was hoping for passing out, but I never did until after I reached the hospital. I have no recollection of having my stomach pumped.

They transferred me to the psychiatric hospital. The first time I was only in ten days. Nobody actually asked me why I'd done it, but they put me on anti-depressants as well as the valium, and sent me home again. The kids were still in care. I saw Craig once a week, with David. I didn't see the other two. Mostly I was in contact with them by phone. Sometimes I took Craig for a meal in town or to the pictures. The kids only knew I hadn't been well. With Craig, there weren't so many crises at this time, or if there were, I was shielded from them. There was lots of help then. For me. I attended the hospital. I had a psychiatric nurse once a week. I saw the doctor. I saw the psychiatrist. I was on valium. I was on anti-depressants. But no one was taking on Craig as the problem. As far as they were concerned I had had a breakdown and my kids had gone into care. That's still how it is.

Sometimes I was coping. Sometimes I wasn't coping at all. I didn't have much of a relationship with Craig. The wee one was missing me. I felt a total failure as a mother. An absolute total failure. I wasn't sleeping. In the end I didn't sleep for a whole week. I was feeling suicidal again. I was a zombie. I was desperate for sleep and I couldn't. So they took me back into hospital. I was in for seven weeks. They took me off the medication. And I plummeted. I wouldn't be able to find my room. My concentration was away again. I had to write everything down. And believe it or not, the most important thing to me, always, was to remember to phone Craig when I promised I was going to. One night I had drawn this great big telephone, and I'd written, 'Remember to phone Craig'. But I forgot. I was in such a state it took three nurses to try to calm me down. And I'm saying, 'No, my son will not understand. I promised my son. If I can't stick by the very simple things I promise him, he's going to feel let down.' In the end one of the nurses phoned Craig's foster parent to explain why I hadn't phoned, and it was the next day I was supposed to phone. It wasn't that day at all.

I was getting worse. It got to the point I was having hourly conversations with David about why I shouldn't kill myself. He was brilliant. I would not be here if it wasn't for that man. Definitely not. I would have killed myself.

I should have shouted louder at the beginning. After years of contact with social workers, I know how to play them now.

Now I don't say, 'I don't think I can cope with this. I'm finding this difficult.' I say, 'I AM NOT COPING.' I spent a year going up and down to Social Work before Craig was finally taken into care. I was saying, 'I don't understand this boy. Will somebody help me with this boy,' and they were saying, 'And what are your politics? And what is your relationship with David? And you're a single parent, aren't you?' And I was saying, 'It's my son, my son, my son. I am not the problem. It's my son who is the problem.' They never listened to me and they never believed me. All that energy which was focused on me could have gone into trying to identify what was going on with Craig. But no. It has taken me years to get them to finally admit he has behavioural problems. Only now they've tried living with Craig do they know how difficult and tiring and wearing he can be. Even his foster parent says how tired she is after a few hours with Craig. They should try five years – twenty-four hours a day for long periods each time he was excluded from school. I was stuck with that problem for too long, on my own. It's taken five years and my sanity to get them to admit that he has problems. Craig's fifteen now. He's on drugs. He has a criminal record. I don't see him. Recently I've asked him not even to phone me.

Now I can acknowledge that the relationship between me and my son broke down over many years. I am salvaging what I can. I've not given up on him. Things are becoming clearer – now that we are apart. I feel bad about it. I feel crap. I'm his mum and I want to be his mum, but he won't let me. So it's still ongoing. It will always be ongoing. It's always going to be a big hurt. It's always going to be something I never got right. Being Craig's mother is something that will never end.

Double Edged

Emma Marx

This edginess
most parents
don't know

that doorbell ring
a son breaking a door
hand on a gun

*'let me in
you have to'*

If he came to hide
you could take that
but he's shouting

and his hand wobbles
on the safety

will he swallow
medication

or this time
will you fall

Calling 911
complaints to police
do no good

he's your son

Staying on the Same Side

Kate Cargreaves

Last week, without warning, I found myself aching for the six-year-old with whom I had such a joyful, spontaneous closeness. Life then was so simple. Tom was at school, and I was no longer exhausted by his day-long, manic energy. But he was still a lovable, loving *child*: dependent enough to satisfy my maternal desires, and yet independent enough to leave me space for myself. I vividly remember wanting to stop time, so that he would never grow up. One night I dreamed of looking at small shoes in a shop, sad that they would not fit my son. He was no longer my little boy.

Tom is now thirteen – going on sixteen. He is athletically good looking, towers over me and wears size ten shoes. His physical development and outbreak of spots herald the arrival of puberty. His attitude screams out hormonal overload! He has always been strong-willed, but life for us has become an emotional roller coaster. Our home is a territorial battlefield. Gigantic skates bar the door to the fridge, soggy towels routinely litter the bathroom floor; dirty underwear is strewn across the landing. He seeks to provoke, asks constantly for money we don't have, and reduces me to crumpled exhaustion by his moods, his jungle music, his refusal to go to bed at night – followed by his stubborn immovability on school mornings.

Oversized boys drenched in Lynx drop their bikes across our doorway, wander in and out of our home, skate around the kitchen. He struts his stuff, shouts to me 'Slave! Fetch me a drink!' It's a non-starter and he knows it; they just enjoy the entertainment of my lectures on sexism. They laugh at me for suggesting they should wear cycle helmets: squashed heads are the stuff of their casual jokes, not a real threat involving brain-damage or death. I age each time Tom goes out.

The chaos in his room I can just about bear. He's always been anarchic. The notice on his door says, 'This is the place where clothes come to die!' Every few days I scoop up an armful of jeans and T-shirts, and wash them whether they need it or not. Otherwise I mostly ignore it.

The state of his furniture is another matter. The graffiti is quite a work of art. But he's taken to cutting up his room with his penknife. The chips in his cheap cabin bed aren't so bad: the duvet hides them. But now he has started on the bookcase. We can't afford to replace furniture as he wrecks it. I 'throw a wobbly' as he puts it.

There must be a *reason* for these acts of vandalism. What was he *feeling* when he chipped at his furniture? But how do you get an adolescent boy to talk about feelings? I have to try. After yet another scene I knock on the door of his room. He lies scowling on the bed, refusing to acknowledge me. I am learning the hard way that I always have to make the first move. Pride or principle must be abandoned. I just have to get on in there and break the ice – and never to be afraid to say 'sorry' if it's my fault. I'm also learning to save my energies for the big battles and give way over the small.

It takes time and endless patience, but in the end he says he always cuts up his furniture after a scene with his dad or me.

He comes up with the surprisingly insightful explanation that, 'It gets the tension out of me.'

I work hard at keeping the lines of communication open. At last we get somewhere. One thing becomes clear: he feels that the boundaries we set him are wholly unfair and that he should have the same freedoms as an adult. Thirty years on, I can empathise with my own mother, whom I had secretly blamed for mishandling me at the same age. Is it just possible that I was as unreasonable at thirteen as my son?

Eventually I manage to unearth some of the anger and confusion that is caged in this boy-man frame. We reach some semblance of understanding and accommodation. Cutting up his furniture has to stop. The penknife is confiscated. I suggest he try to *talk to me* when he's feeling enraged. The art of meaningful conversation, though, is a bit subtle for him at present.

Resolution brings a sense of achievement. There is, though, little time to congratulate myself for my diplomacy: no sooner is one problem sorted than another takes its place as Tom fights to reassert control. The latest battle is getting him up for school. Tempers are inevitably frayed when tired adults try to rouse a mutely defiant teenager and get him out at the start of the working day. This is not just perverseness on Tom's part: he is dyslexic, so academic work is especially arduous for him. At his most unreasonable or desperate he feels that school is a complete waste of time. Larger class sizes and stressed-out teachers simply cannot meet his educational needs. Endless hours are spent in contact with school and discussion with Tom's private dyslexia tutor. My determination that he will not slip through the net is absolute. I tell myself he'll thank me one day. But it's a huge struggle and I only cope by creating my own network of support.

There is an extra dimension to our relationship, which has become more significant as Tom matures. He is adopted. I have been his mother since he was ten weeks old, and I can't imagine loving any son borne of my own body any more than

I love him. I sometimes wonder whether, when we row, he ever thinks about me as 'not my real mother'. There is no doubt that being adopted makes him feel insecure and influences his behaviour. No amount of unconditional love can fully heal the wound of separation from his birth mother, and the knowledge that she chose to give him up.

This has become more apparent as Tom deals with questions about identity which are common in adolescence, but particularly momentous for adopted people. Painful as it is for us, he is entitled to his feelings about his origins and I have always been honest with him. A few months ago I re-discovered an envelope of mementos and photos of his birth mother as a child. He'd never wanted to see them before, but this time he did.

He sat on the rug in tears as he looked at the girl who, at the age of seventeen, was to give birth to him. For the first time he saw someone who looked like him. The following hour was wrenchingly sad, as he wept silently and helplessly – my macho son, weeping for the woman who had given him life, and for the loss of her.

He was ready, then, for the letter about his beginnings which his social worker had given us in trust after his adoption. The depth of his suffering cut my heart, yet he needed me to be there and share with him in it. Afterwards, he wanted his mum to make cocoa and toast and honey. I felt we had shared an emotional milestone and, though drained, was proud and thankful.

He took possession of the envelope of photos and stuck it on his bedroom wall. It is there still, though appears untouched. But it is his, and available to him if he needs it. I can only affirm him in his right to feel pain and loss and longing. If, when he is eighteen, he wishes to search for his birth mother, I hope to have the strength to support and help him. Yes, I wish I had carried Tom and given birth to him, but I feel privileged to have been entrusted with him, and profoundly grateful to the young woman who made it possible.

I still crumbled, though, when he asked me to buy him a locket so that he could have 'a picture of my mum' in it. I thought he meant me. I recoiled at the use of the word 'mum' to describe the woman I had always distanced by calling her Tom's 'birth mother'. 'I'm your mum!' I whimpered. Tom ran upstairs and sobbed behind a locked bathroom door. For the first time ever I felt totally unable to help him. For a couple of days after this my security as an adoptive mother was shaken to the core. It was only with the support of an adoption worker who is herself adopted that I was able to confront my deepest feelings and to accept Tom's right to some sort of closeness, if only through a photograph, with the person to whom he is so irreversibly and profoundly related.

In all the years of Tom's life I have never suggested he is 'lucky' to be with us. Sometimes others say this of adopted children. *We* are the lucky ones; a loving home and family is every child's birthright. But such are the pressures of life with our adolescents that recently I broke my cardinal rule.

Tom has always resented his younger sister. She came to us as a vulnerable two-year-old and still needs extra reassurance to boost her self-esteem. Tom had almost seven years as the long-awaited, adored only child. He has always considered it his god-given right to have more of everything than her, including my attention.

In adolescence he has increasingly used her as a dumping ground for his own insecurities. He and his friends repeatedly give her the impression that boys are more powerful and more entitled. I am determined that she will not grow up feeling inferior because she is a girl.

Once, when yet again his behaviour to his sister broke all bounds, I exploded. I told him angrily how lucky he is to have such a good home and family, and that, if he has any fantasies about how life would be with his birth mother, he is a damn sight better off here! I also told him, with no holds barred, that I had enough love for both my children, and that it was time he stopped resenting his sister for being here.

After delivering these home truths I was ashamed. I have, I believe, always tackled my children's adoptions with skill and insight: how could I blow it all in one overheated moment? Tom, however, took it in his stride. He was much nicer, and full of good cheer, after the dust settled. Mothers are only human and adolescents can be surprisingly tolerant. My son is wilful and self-obsessed at times but he can also be wonderfully kind and gentle if I am really distressed.

There is a lot of conflict in our home as Tom goes through a particularly complex adolescence and there is no short cut through it. We bear the brunt of his moods and demands, but slowly and surely we are working things through. He has a strong hunger for street cred, and at times I feel terrifyingly powerless to shield him from the potential allure of sex, drugs and criminal activity. His father and I work ceaselessly to teach him values which we can only trust he accepts at heart. And while I often despair over his behaviour, I know that really he is a lovely lad. Humour is our lifeline. We have masses of fun together, lolling on the settee watching TV, acting the fool and laughing like drains. He is a tremendously positive person, too, and his sporting prowess fills me with delight. Despite all the pressures, he is a source of supreme pride.

Earlier, I spotted him through the window with his friends, out on the street. They were probably saying things unfit for adult consumption, but I felt intense joy as I secretly watched my popular, fun-loving, attractive son. For a moment I entirely forgot the stresses of navigating him through the stormy seas of adolescence and into maturity. As long as we can, somehow, stay on the same side, I am hopeful that we will make it. And manage to have plenty of laughter along the way.

So Many Voices

Jiffy Sandison

1.

'Hi there, it's me – Rachel.'

'Oh! I've been meaning to phone you . . .' I reply.

'I'd almost given you up for lost! Are you okay?'

'Well, you know . . . so, so.'

'Is it Douglas?'

'Yeah.'

'I thought it was. I said to Mary – I can't think why she hasn't phoned for so long . . . What's he done now?'

'Not a lot.'

I can picture him in the next bedroom as we speak. A large Black adolescent with a mop of wild plaits shooting up from a shaved head. He's reclining on his bed surrounded by dirty food plates, upturned glasses and empty Coca-cola bottles. I can hear both the television and his stereo playing relentless rap music. On his chair is the residue of stubbed out cigarette butts waiting to be relit for a maximum nicotine rush. The curtains are closed, the room in its usual smoky fug. The only light is the flickering screen which he keeps on all night.

'The last time we spoke he was going to that unit in September. How's he doing?'

'He refused to go . . .'

'Refused!' Rachel's disapproval sets my stomach churning. 'How could he . . . he's only sixteen?'

'He's a big lad, I can't physically throw him out of the door.'

I remember shouting at him as he stood immobile in his room, 'There's nowhere else to go after this . . . This is the end of the line! Do you hear me?'

'I don't care, I'd rather die than do the journey through that area.' He held his ground, his chin thrust out and his lips trembling.

'So what does he do all day?'

'Sleeps most of the time, I believe.'

'I hope he gets the tea on at least. There's you working hard all day, the cheek of him!'

Rachel's known me since Douglas was a toddler. She means well, but she makes it sound so simple. He ought to go to school, he ought to do his share, he ought to toe the line. I ought to ensure that he does. What I can't bear is we both know it's not like that. If it were that simple, why do we hear so many tales of parents driven mad by their teenagers!

'You've got to talk to him, make him see sense!'

Talk to him! What does she think I've been doing all the time? I've spent bitter hours outside his locked bedroom door alternately cajoling or screaming.

'Come on, Douglas. Nothing's ever as bad as you fear, love! If you go to the unit where the pressure isn't too much, you'll build your confidence. Honestly, I'm not bothered about you passing exams, I just want you to get out of your room.'

His silence is exaggerated by the thumping base of the stereo.

'Douglas, turn that blasted thing off and come out here right now. If you don't co-operate with me I'll . . .'

'What'll you do?' Douglas growls through the door.

'Don't you get mad?' Rachel demands. 'I wouldn't put up with it, I'd probably kill him if he was mine.'

'I'm afraid I don't often feel angry nowadays, just despairing.'

'Don't say that, it's not all your fault. What about his dad? He's more to blame . . . leaving it all to you.'

'Don't worry, Rachel, we'll get by. It's nice of you to phone.'

'Let me know what happens, please. You're doing a great job really, we all think so.'

I've had quite a few of those telephone conversations. They take about two days to get over. I've tried most of the solutions they suggest, I have agonised over a stream of worst scenarios that keep me awake at night. Such friends give me the additional burden of their anxiety. Their unvoiced accusation that I'm being too soft feeds into an overflowing well of guilt at my sense of failure as a parent.

2.

My partner calls it the 'Hampstead model of child-rearing'. He characterises it as the child having limitless needs and rights and the parent having none.

I always clashed with my husband over Douglas' upbringing. There's nothing like an alien view to crystallise your own.

I remember one morning when Douglas was eighteen months old.

'Make sure he has his porridge,' my husband commanded on his way out to work. 'Oh, and you should get that Seven Seas cod liver oil for him. We don't want him catching a cold.'

'It's okay,' I replied with a sleepy tot in my arms. 'I've got new blackcurrant multi-vitamins. They're the same only they taste nice. Douglas thinks they're sweeties!'

My husband wrinkled his dark brown nose. 'That's no good, it's not meant to taste nice. My mother brought us up on cod liver oil in Africa and what's good enough for me's good enough for him!'

He kissed us both and left me to carry out instructions.

My ex-husband came from a religious home with clear ideas about parenting and life in general. There was one way to do things – his way! If you posed another model, you had better be very sure of your ground.

'Come on, Douglas, eat some porridge for Mummy,' I cajoled half-heartedly. The pursed lips clamped shut and his head shook to and fro. 'Just another mouthful,' I made the noise of a descending plane as I directed the spoon in circular flight towards him.

I was too late to catch the bowl of porridge thrown with great strength across the room. Douglas chuckled delightedly as arcs of grey goo splashed cupboards. The upturned bowl and remaining contents landed under the cooker in amongst the grease and fluff.

Douglas was a very large baby; the product of another piece of certainty – 'babies cannot be overfed on the breast.' By four months he was almost spherical and still I suckled him on demand.

The last thing my son needed at fifteen months was porridge. He needed to eat less. He needed a bit of fruit. He needed to go on a diet! That's why he kept chucking porridge at me. He was more aware of his body's requirements than his father or I were.

The trouble with opposing my husband's certainty was that at any one time I had about five voices in my head. I had been brought up with liberal reasoning as a household god. Any argument deserved a counter-argument.

–'Douglas needs porridge like a hole in the head.'

–'Yes, but it's important his father has a say in his upbringing.'

–'How can I administer something I've no faith in?'

–'If my husband thinks it's such a good idea, he can give it himself . . .'

–'If I fight my husband over small things it will destroy our marriage. What's a bowl of porridge against a divorce?'

We fought over a lot more than porridge in the end. Now I didn't have to fight his rigid view of childrearing. Yippee!

3.

But what was my view of child-rearing? What was my voice? That wasn't so easy and it remains difficult. I've still got those conflicting voices in my head, but now they are joined by all those voices 'out there', the opinions I have sought out or absorbed as I struggled to raise my child on my own.

–'Children need boundaries and consistency.'

–'Single parents are the cause of all these problem children.'

–'We have underestimated the terrible damage that divorce has on a growing child.'

At least I managed to hold down a job and hide some of my more notable failures within the privacy of my own home. I was a teacher and very good at looking after other people's children. And I parried any well-meaning questions with platitudes.

'How's that son of yours doing at school? He's in secondary now, isn't he?'

'Oh, you know, he's taking a while to settle in. It's quite a change from primary for some children, isn't it?'

But the day came when my two worlds collided and my guilty secret was out.

'I've got a visitor in my room,' the Deputy told me over the phone. 'He's come quite a long way to see you.' The amusement in her voice gave the game away.

'Is it my son?'

'Yes, he's all right, I kept him in my office while you were teaching. Can you come and get him?'

I dashed down between lessons to find a penitent eleven-year-old.

'You told me to come to you if I lost my temper,' he

snivelled. 'I've run away . . . I hate that school. I want to go back to my primary.'

From then he ran away on a regular basis. He'd chosen the school, and some of his classmates had gone up with him, but he didn't adjust to the new setting.

'I don't like my tutor; she said she could tell I was naughty just by looking at me. And she shouts,' Douglas sulked.

How many times did I hear tales like that? Douglas had the idea that 'somewhere over the rainbow' was the perfect school for him. I had forgotten to instil in him the concept of grinning and bearing it.

If I had my chance again, I would be tougher with Douglas about schools. I wouldn't take his terrible protestations so seriously, I'd tell him to take the rough with the smooth, I'd . . .

But some things you must take seriously as a parent. How are you to know which things?

4.

'Come quickly, Douglas's been raped in the cemetery . . . hurry up!'

Somehow I made it to the local green where I found an ambulance, police cars, the local youth workers and the teenage 'posse' to which Douglas belonged.

Douglas' face was covered with scratches, his nose was swollen – it looked like it had been broken. He was standing very stiffly, his face impassive. I ran to him and put out my arms; he held me with a new awkwardness. He was trembling uncontrollably.

'Bastard!' he growled. 'Bastard! I'll kill him!'

Hours later I discovered he hadn't actually been raped. He'd been jumped by an older kid – a complete stranger.

The boy had beaten Douglas severely and tried to remove his trousers. He hadn't taken any money. It seemed a senseless act.

This incident lost Douglas two years of his life. At first he went back to school but as time went on he became nervous about setting foot outside the door. He refused to travel alone; for a while he wouldn't even walk down the road to the local shops.

'You don't know what it's like for Black youths now – it's not like your old days!' Douglas screamed at me once.

'But it was a Black kid that attacked you!'

'So!' he yelled. 'When I pass a white woman in the street she jumps away from me and grabs onto her bag. Imagine what that feels like! You've got to be on your guard all the time. You've no idea!'

5.

'But he's missed so much of his studies,' says Rachel. 'Such a bright boy and you a teacher!'

Funnily enough I'm not worried about that, I'm much more concerned that he gets out there and deals with the world.

'What kind of job's he going to get? It's such a waste.'

'People can always go back to education – if Douglas chooses to, he'll take up learning later.'

'I don't know how you put up with it. Even if he was mugged, that was ages ago. Lots of children get attacked and get over it, what's so special about Douglas?'

The other day I came home from school to find Douglas with his posse. They greeted me gruffly then went back into his room; he locked his door as usual.

Minutes later they stomped along the corridor and slammed the door behind them. 'I know where he's gone with them, off to buy some fags – bloody kids!'

Five minutes later I heard his lone trainers dragging along the corridor. The kitchen door burst open. There he stood before me with his hands behind his back – a tall, chubby, boy-man, voluminous trousers tucked in at the ankle and barely covering his cheeks at the back, a black, stained T-shirt with cigarette burn marks.

Suddenly his arm shot out from behind his back and proffered a bunch of flowers, unwrapped and dripping with water.

He smiled shyly, 'I didn't know what you're supposed to get.' He shuffled. 'The guys said flowers, so here they are. Happy Mother's Day!'

At Home in the Living Room

Hazell Hills

He retires, after an exam he says was crap, to hunch in front of
the television. Tomorrow, he knows — and I, his mother, know
— brings yet another A Level he's not revised for. His older
sister, A–levelled last year, sits apart, chain–migrained, out–of–
work for months.

> Outside
> Two pigeons free–fall,
> the sky transparent through their pantiled wing–tips
> before they slot
> into an airstream
> to let themselves be drawn away.
>
> Twilight makes outside the backdrop.
> In here is the scene:
> The Unities are not observed;
> There is no plot
> No purpose
> No purposeful purposelessness
> so that we can say
> 'Ah, this is just like Beckett' or
> 'Here is Ionesco's Theatre of the Absurd'.
>
> It is nothing
> that can be
> packaged, labelled or conveniently contained.
> They are it.
> It is them.
>
> I cannot see a yellow–brick road
> apparent in this set,
> no rainbowed cyclorama.
> No permanent right of way.
>
> And there is no intermission.

Shopping, The Big Event, and The Cycle Helmet

Helen Braid

1. SHOPPING

I am walking the required three paces behind pretending, as instructed, that I do not know him. I am not related to him. I have never seen him before in my life. Occasionally I am rewarded with a backward look, a glowering frown. We are (God help me!) shopping for clothes for *him*.

I just wish I had thought of it sooner. Jogging trousers. For the past eight weeks, on Thursday mornings, I have scanned my brain for another plausible reason why my son can not do PE wondering, as I write, if these documents are grounds for jail. My son has had flu. Three times. Has fallen off his bike. Has had a bad migraine. The dog bit him. There was an unexploded mine at the bottom of the garden. And so on. Because his legs are the wrong shape and he will suffer torment from the other kids if they see the light of day. My son is six foot and eight stone. My heart aches for him because

I've been there too. Last week I ran out of excuses, and the PE teacher ran out of patience. My son reports that he is going to be ill with the man's ranting and raging. Well, that at least would solve the problem.

I signal to the turned back that we try the sports shop but no, we must enter the torture chamber. I try to cast a protective circle round myself — against the mega-decibels of hammering pop, the headache-producing lights, the whirls and swirls of cheap tat. And the salesman whose hands have slipped with the after-shave. I have been instructed not to speak unless our lives are threatened. I must not smile. I must not say that this stuff will fall to bits on its first encounter with the washing machine. I must not speak the designer labels out loud because last time I pronounced 'Nike' wrong. And everybody heard. He could not survive another such humiliation.

I try hand signals to indicate that there are loads of jogging trousers in the sale. Half-price. But his antennae wave him unerringly to the only items which cost my year's clothing allowance. They are different. They are essential. He would not be seen dead in anything else. The chosen joggers have a tiny little word sewn on one leg and two tiny green stripes on the other. This is VERY IMPORTANT. Anyone (except his mother) knows this.

The salesman is doing his best, handing more and more pairs of identical black joggers to the snapping turtle behind the curtains. My son has indicated that I stand motionless nearby. If I take so much as a step towards the cubicle, he will hiss and tug the curtain half off its rail. Not a crack of light must be left in case somebody (especially, Heaven help him, his mother) sees him. I am not allowed to see the item on. I try to forget that the last pair of jeans he bought after similar torment did not reach his ankles. We had to come back and do it all again.

I fantasise about a chair and some iced water. I fantasise about not having a teenage son at all. I have been waiting near the entrance, longing to put my fingers in my ears, for a very long time. Then at last, at long last, I receive the signal to rush to the till with my cheque-book ready. Despite the fact that he has taken half-an-hour, I must be very very quick. I must not examine the goods, must not comment on his choice, must not show a glimmer of shock at the price-tag. Above all, I must not act in any way like a mother.

I pay up, and he stalks out leaving me to follow three paces behind, carrying the bag.

2. THE BIG EVENT

The back door is flung open – and left open so that the dogs escape and the cold air blasts in – and my son, plus Stuart, Benjy, and Peter, troop past. They are not slouching, nor complaining about the tediousness and eternal boredom of their cruelly inflicted rural existence. They are self-important. They are deep in agitated top-level planning. This is a summit meeting. They grab the cordless phone and rush into my son's room. The green light of the base unit in the kitchen flickers on and off. On and off. They are phoning half the world. I call the dogs and shut the back door.

Five minutes later they are back.

'We're going up the village to get James,' I am informed as they all troop out again.

Ten minutes later my son and four different boys troop down the garden path, leave the door open, strut through the kitchen, and use the phone for a further fifteen minutes. I shut the door. They re-emerge.

'We're going back up the village to get Lee.'

It takes a while to find the dogs.

For the next hour and a half this scene is re-enacted many times. Our kitchen is by now very cold and the dogs are missing. Half-way through the morning the boys, looking embarrassed and overjoyed, are accompanied by a *girl*. This, you must appreciate, is a rare event as the boys are only fourteen or younger and usually not worthy of her interest. She uses our phone to ring all her private school friends.

The boys are back for the tenth time, hot, sweating and exhausted from climbing and re-climbing the steep hill to the village to discuss and arrange the evening's entertainment. My son mutters something about tents, sausages, cider, out-all-night, and VERY IMPORTANT. I can only understand about a fifth of what he says to me these days. I maintain that he mumbles. He says I'm deaf. Someone has found the button in his back which I, his mother, fail to locate every morning when I need to get him out of bed and ready for school. He is wound up like a clockwork mouse on pills. 'We've got to get ready *now*. We're having a camping party and *everyone's* coming from town. About forty or fifty people. It's all arranged.'

He is jubilant. He is exultant, and I understand that this is indeed a major coup. The townies have apparently agreed to come all the way out to our rural dump instead of breathing the evening carbon monoxide of the city centre. Townie boys and townie girls. From my son's state school, and posh private ones. They are coming, hordes of them, with rucksacks and sleeping bags and booze to sample the novelty of a rural rave.

It is 2 p.m. The attic hatch is open, the back and front doors are open, the dogs have probably been taken into care, and in the kitchen, in a heap, are tents, potatoes, my frying pan, my olive oil, all my matches, marshmallows, bacon, bottles of cider and the ghetto-blaster. I have driven twice to the local shops to buy the necessary junk food. The wheelbarrow is brought into commission and forays up the field begin. This is hard, hard work. Every few minutes the phone rings. Village teenagers gather in my son's room.

'Where are my new jeans and my black top?' my son demands, boss to secretary.

'On your bedroom floor dirty where you left them, I expect.'

'I need them *now*.'

'But you're only camping.'

'You don't understand, do you? You've not been listening. You never listen. This is REALLY IMPORTANT.'

As I start up the washing machine for two lone items, I worry about the ozone layer and imagine the hundreds of Bacchanalian youths who will soon be stampeding through the night in this tiny-minded little village of ours.

The labourers are resting. They are not used to this kind of physical exertion. It is three in the afternoon and they look shattered. I sense a slight drooping of spirits as they slump in front of the video. The phone is still in constant use and I am informed that parents are manning the Volvos ready to ferry out the teenage population. Plans seem fluid as the timing of the start of the event changes from seven to eight to nine. Then back to seven again. It starts to rain.

At six o'clock my son wets his hair and combs it flat on his head until he resembles Ratty. He puts on his jeans – still warm from the tumble-dryer – and his new expensive dready-top. He is fizzing with anxiety, anticipation and excitement.

At six-thirty, five village boys set off up the hill pushing the remaining gear in the wheelbarrow.

At nine-thirty, my son is back for some forgotten item.

'How's it going?' I ask.

'It's not started yet. They're not here yet. Parties don't start till about ten. We're not babies.'

I go to bed at midnight, too exhausted to listen out any more for the sounds of an all-night thrash. I'm sure my neighbours or the police will be round soon enough if it gets out of hand.

At nine the next morning, my son and one mate appear in the kitchen doorway. They are crumpled, damp, and ashen. It must have been quite a party.

'How did it go then? How many turned up? Did you have a good time?' I've got into this silly habit of asking strings of questions in the hope that maybe my son will deign to reply to one of them.

'*No one* came,' he snarls as he stomps off to bed. 'They've got better things to do than to come all the way out to a fucking dump like this! Peter and me slept in the tent.'

Oh, my poor son! What wasted energy. What pointless exhaustion. How many more times must it happen like this before you learn?

I haven't the heart to ask him to fetch my frying pan so that the rest of the family can have our usual Sunday pancakes for breakfast.

3. THE CYCLE HELMET

My son is arguing about wearing his cycle helmet. Three of his buddies are standing in the doorway watching us spar.

Recently I seem to be losing a lot of these little domestic battles. I have weakened on a number of issues which he regards as matters for the European Court of Human Rights. Like staying out until 2 a.m. Like eating a choc-ice for breakfast. Like living in a room which resembles the aftermath of the Glastonbury Festival. Like using our entire supply of towels in a week and leaving them wet on the floor. Like being paid a working man's weekly wage just for cleaning my car. Inadequately.

But about wearing his skid-lid – I know I am right.

Apparently it is not cool to wear a cycle helmet. Only nerds do it. The three non-nerds nod in agreement. Anyway he is only going up the lane to the village. It's only a tiny country road. Cars hardly ever materialise on it. How could he possibly fall off just pottering about with his mates? He is barely going to leave the tracks of the fields. He *knows* how to ride his bike. What do I think he is? An amateur? His cycle helmet makes him too hot. His cycle helmet spoils his hair. His cycle helmet is, if anything, a danger because it gives him 'a false sense of security' and forces him to take risks he would not take when not wearing it. *None* of his friends wear a cycle helmet. I am being really stupid. I am being *totally unreasonable*. I am the only mother in the whole world who would dream of making such a fool of her son.

Trying to ignore the sneers from the doorway, and my son's

eyes raised to the heavens in disbelief that I should disagree with him in front of his friends, I harness my arguments:

1. It is not his cycling skills I am worried about but those of the car drivers.
2. It only takes one car to knock him off his bike.
3. It is possible to come off a bike on any road — even a tiny country road.
4. I have done my homework (groans and more eye-rolling) and know the statistics about injuries to cyclists with and without helmets.
5. I have been round Astlie Ainslie hospital and have seen with my own eyes the tragic consequences of teenagers who have been knocked off their bikes.

I have gone *too far*. I have got too heavy and the other lads are departing. They shake their heads in sympathy with my son. My son points out my total insensitivity.

In any case I cannot force him to wear his helmet.

I can.

I can not. He will wear it to the brow of the hill where my vision peters out and then he will chuck it in the hedge until the return journey.

I will find out.

How?

I just will. If I hear from a single soul that he has been seen riding his bike without his helmet I will ground him. I will confiscate his bike.

I am screaming like a fish-wife and my son is peddling away. Without his skid-lid.

Later the same evening

My son appears in the kitchen doorway. My first thought is that he has been involved in a terrorist attack. His face is covered in blood and his ear seems to be hanging off. He can barely walk. He collapses on the kitchen floor. But before passing out he manages to shout, 'It's all your fault! This would never have happened if you hadn't made such a fuss about the fucking helmet. I only came off because I was thinking about all the stupid things you said!!'

Much later still that night

I am in the accident hospital. My son is writhing as the nice young doctor examines him. He has mild concussion. His ear needs to be stitched back on. His shoulder is dislocated. His wrist is sprained. But he has not cracked his skull and he is still alive. He has to explain that he fell off his bike on a tiny country road. He has to admit that a car coming too fast in the opposite direction made him swerve. He lost his balance. He came off and landed on his head. The village GP scraped him off the road and escorted him back home. He forgets to explain to the doctor that it is all my fault. Falling off his bike has given him selective amnesia.

The nice young doctor is giving my son a lecture about wearing his cycle helmet:
1. It is not necessarily the cyclist's skills but . . .
etc., etc.

My son manages to nod in agreement.

Two weeks later

Glancing out of the window at a sudden burst of sunshine, I notice my son and his mates cycling up the hill. None of them are wearing their crash helmets.

Beauty Sleep:
a Factional Fairytale

Hazell Hills

My Dearest Aurora,

This letter is strictly for your eyes only. As is the enclosure. (The Lord Chamberlain is arranging for the separate despatch of the Royal Christening Robe − and the gold mug and porringer. Just in case you'd thought I'd forgotten! They should arrive in good time for the ceremony.) Only a month today! I am so looking forward to holding Florabella again, the dear, wee pet. She looks just like you did at that age − same eyes, same ears, same hair − or lack of it!)

I send the enclosure solely out of concern for your well-being, my dearest daughter. I would not want you − or anyone − to go through what I have been through. My one, secret aim in life for some years now has been to find a way to make life easier for mothers when their children pass through adolescence.

It was when your father set up a Memorial Fund to Verity (do you remember his Trust to encourage the youth of our realm to accomplish Deeds of Derring Do?) that I got the idea of creating a motherhood society, so secret that only the actual members in it knew of its existence.

With this letter, I send you the only copy of the Inaugural Address which I delivered to the small, carefully selected audience of mothers of teenagers soon after the death of our dear Verity. Please study this address now – before you read the rest of my letter to you.

Ladies.

Thank you all so much for coming to this inaugural meeting of the Mothers Only Royal Federation – to be referred to hereafter as MORF. I feel that I should give you some background information as to why I have asked you personally – and individually – to come here today for this meeting.

You all know, I'm sure, the story which the popular media of the day dubbed 'The Sleeping Beauty'. How my dear daughter Aurora received all those lovely presents at her christening from the Good Fairies – and how the King and I had omitted to invite one fairy, who gate-crashed the royal occasion and put a spell on our beloved daughter, so that, if she ever injured herself and blood flowed, she would die (later commuted to her and the whole realm sleeping for a hundred years).

And how no one wanted this to happen – not her royal parents, not the Court, not the palace servants, not the loyal subjects, etc., etc. And how any work or pastime involving the use of a sharp instrument was immediately banned throughout the kingdom. All this to no avail: at the age of thirteen she pricks herself on the spindle of a spinning wheel. I do not need to tell you the rest of the story: we all know it only too well.

Like much information passed down by word of mouth, this tale has changed in the telling – and I must confess to you that *I* have played a considerable role in this. Let me explain how this came about.

As mothers, you can all probably imagine how I felt when my firstborn, the beloved Princess Verity, was placed in my arms. My delight as I gazed at her fingers with their doll-size tiny nails. My joy as I stroked her downy cheek and she instinctively turned her little head and nuzzled, mouth open, searching for my breast. Oh, the fierce, deep, protective love that welled up in me! I'd never known quite so strong an emotion before. And my happiness, mingled with anxiety, as I cared for her — this dear, dependent being. And then to watch her toddling. To encourage her to speak her first words. How could any of us forget these emotions too deep for expression?

Everything was fine. Even teething, tantrums and the Troublesome Twos lasted no more than a few months. She soon started her schooling and I looked forward to sharing the years ahead with her as she grew into womanhood.

This was when things started to go wrong. Dear little Verity, always so open with me, so enthusiastic about everything — her lessons, her play — so full of happy high spirits — this dear little girl altered practically overnight at the age of thirteen and became an uncommunicative, sloppy, awkward, rude changeling.

I could do nothing right, in her eyes. The uncommunicative bit didn't upset me as much as the rest. I mean, I became quite grateful much of the time when she *didn't* say anything because most of what she *did* say either resulted in an argument, or I'd give in to her immediately just for the sake of peace and quiet — and then I'd feel furious with her for making me feel mad that I'd been weak and had given in to her yet again.

We all of us wanted babies, but which one of us even considered that these babies would, in time, become adolescents? It never crossed my mind once, during all those years when I was first trying to get pregnant, that I might ever wish that I hadn't bothered to do so, or even — and I tell you this in a hushed whisper because it's not the sort of thing that I'd like the media to get hold of — that I quite often wished my teenage child dead. Then, at least, we'd have had a quiet home.

It was the continual questioning of my competence in every area of life that wore me down — as a mother, as a wife, and even as a human being. When you get yourself reflected back as crabby, old-fashioned, mean, indecisive, illogical, bad-tempered, a laughing-stock (I'm sure you can all add to this list from your own experience) there is a great danger that, in your attempt to view things from your adolescent's viewpoint, you can see yourself reacting in exactly the ways that your resident changeling has just so graphically described. And then you feel totally disempowered. Many of you with adolescent sons have told me of equivalent stormy scenes with them.

I have never before been buffeted by such extremes of emotion. Terror. Anguish. Fury. Anxiety. Hate − yes, even hate − of my beloved child. Except she wasn't the beloved child of former years − she was this moody, egocentric monster that saw everything, but everything, in stark black and white. My shades-of-grey version of life she despised. My decisions she questioned: 'Oh, Mum, *everyone else* is allowed to − ' whatever was the subject of contention at that time. I felt out of step with life; powerless; not knowing what to think, what stand to take − or even if I should make a stand. (What if I should lose her forever? What if she left home if I laid down the law? And then sneakily feeling for half a second how blissfully quiet home would be if she did.)

'Mum, can I borrow your hairbrush/hair-dryer/lipstick/tights/new jacket?' (Again, you are all able to continue the list.)

And you are really pleased that she even for one moment considers that some belonging of yours is worth borrowing. 'Yes, dear. Of course,' you say. 'You're welcome to borrow it any time. Just put it back afterwards in my room.'

And does she? We all recognise the ensuing scenario. We also all recognise our own reluctance to set the scene for another showdown, so either we ignore the non-return of our object, or we scuttle guiltily into her room to reclaim our property, having first checked that she's out and so won't catch us there unasked. Guilt is what we're good at.

And yet, through all of this, especially when I'm not the object of her hawklike scrutiny, I feel that fierce protective love for her rise up in my veins when the expected 'phone call from that pimply prince she met recently doesn't happen, or he's due to ride over here on his white charger and he doesn't arrive, while she sits, arrayed in her best outfit, brimful of happy anticipation. I could *kill* him for so upsetting her. Or when her friends break friends with her: my heart aches for her; I feel a lead weight in my stomach. (And yet another part of me is also thinking that it's amazing that she ever has any friends if she behaves towards them as she does at home.)

I've talked with other mothers of adolescents and found that they were going through much the same trauma as I was. We were all at our wits' end.

Had I known what mothering an adolescent would be like, I'd have throttled the baby at birth or stifled it with a Brussels' lace-trimmed royal pillow. Sadly – and inexplicably – infanticide carries a much lighter penalty than adolescenticide.

You can perhaps imagine my overwhelming feelings of guilt and loss when the Princess Verity was suddenly taken from us as the result of a riding accident at the age of eighteen. My husband was very anxious that we should have another child because of the succession to the throne, and so Aurora – or Beauty as she is now more commonly called – arrived a year later.

It was my duty to provide an heir. But there was no way that I was going through that living hell of inhabiting the same building as a teenager again. Something had to be sorted out before she reached the age of puberty.

Now, all women, as we know, are good at doing more than one thing at a time. However, in my case – and here I am going to let you into a big secret – there is an additional boon. A very rare gene exists in our family which allows the owner to be present in more than one place at a time. It's hard to believe, I know, but it's true. (That's also me over there, taking notes.) So at Aurora's christening I was both sitting beside the baby's crib, looking the picture of maternal adoration, and, at the same time, gate-crashing the event in the shape of the uninvited

Wicked Fairy. It was I who arranged, by means of the spell cast on Beauty, that, when she reached adolescence, the whole realm would fall into a deep, lengthy and peaceful sleep. Well, the only viable alternative would have been to have had her removed permanently and that would have been too unpleasant, too final. I just wanted to avoid those ghastly teenage years again; to play for time. So I arranged it that when Beauty awoke she would be twenty years old, while the rest of us wouldn't have aged at all. I also took the precaution of organising events so that the only way we'd all become conscious again was when Beauty had been kissed awake by a handsome prince, who would then marry her and take her off in his royal carriage to live in the next kingdom, where they would live happily ever after.

With the present rapid growth of technology, I foresee a time in the not-too-far-distant future when women will no longer have to be able to do more than one thing at a time or to try to be in more than one place at one time. They may find their ability to do either or both of these atrophies through lack of use.

So it is that I have taken the precaution of setting up a laboratory (entirely staffed by older married women) to investigate the feasibility of using genetic engineering to develop, isolate and replicate a 'Sleeping Beauty' gene. This gene, during a period of deep sleep, would allow the adolescent's body to go through the physical and mental development of the years 13–19 without the accompanying emotional and social traumas suffered by us all at present.

In this way, all mothers could avoid mothering adolescents. What a benefit for womenkind this would be! And the children concerned could go directly – and gently – from childhood to adulthood. Truly, your children would rise up and call you blessed!

It is because this gene has not been easy to locate – though we have at last just done it – that I have invited you ladies here today. For the last eighteen years (excluding the 100 that we have all been unconscious), I have funded the research totally myself. It is because I am no longer financially able to do this that today I turn to you other mothers to ask for your help in the further financing of this project.

You may be wondering why I have not invited any fathers along to this meeting. It is a conscious decision on my part because I feel that few fathers − if any − are involved in parenting to the extent that we women are, so that men's investment in the project would be less and they would be more likely to object to the whole nature of this research, coming up with objections that they would see as over-ridingly important and which we women would view as merely marginal − if relevant at all. Such as the country falling behind in the arms' race and technological advance, during the Long Sleep Periods.

The total secrecy about the research right from the beginning has, I feel, been vital. I was afraid that individuals or other countries could make unscrupulous use of the foreknowledge of our whole nation's undergoing a Long Sleep Period regularly.

Our Research Director, Dr Helen Jones, is here today. I am now throwing the meeting open for questions, which either Dr Jones or I will do our best to answer.

And now you yourself, my dearest daughter, have just become a young mother. Because of my great love for you, I felt that I had to write to you to set the record straight.

That inaugural speech was delivered six years ago and since then the research has developed apace, so much so that only seven years' sleep − possibly less − will be necessary by the time Florabella reaches thirteen, to enable her to slide gently from childhood to twenty years of age.

The latest clinical trials suggest that, within the next twenty years, the application of the research will make it possible for any adolescent to age an extra seven years during a single night's sleep.

Although I have used the feminine form referring to the adolescent throughout my speech and this letter, I am very well aware that all I have written about female teenagers is equally true of the male version.

The covering letter that you sent me with the invitation to Florabella's christening was full of your concern about not omitting anyone of importance from the guest list – in case there was a repeat performance of what happened at *your* christening. I am still just as capable of being in two places simultaneously and would be very happy to arrange that, in thirteen years' time, everyone in your kingdom takes a seven-year nap and that during that time only Florabella would age.

Two cases of Sleeping-Beauty-itis in our family might trigger more media coverage than we would want at this point, so if you decide to take up my offer, you might need to feed your Palace Press Officer the tale that there are certain rare recessive genes in your family's maternal line, one of which – once in the lifetime of the carrier – predisposes him/her and the rest of the realm to a long sleep. You could mention how haemophilia runs in some royal families and blind the PPO with a bit of science by using such phrases as "the DNA molecular structure and its chemical sequence", "synthesis of body proteins", "neurotransmitters", "PMT and hormonal reactions". That should give him something to think about!

By the time Florabella is a mother and has a twelve-year-old, the overnight-aging genetic engineering should be available to all in the form of a gene replacement at the zygote stage.

Darling, just let me know if you'd like me to do my Double Act at the christening next month. I'd be very happy to oblige. If you use E-mail to reply, make no mention of any of the above, just include "Sleep well" somewhere in your communication.

Oceans of love, as always,

MUM

XXX

PS Please kiss the Dear Wee Pet for me – right on the nape of her neck.

Contributors' Notes

Jane Allan was born in Forres, Morayshire in 1953. She has three sons of 18, 15 and 5 and lives with her partner on a smallholding in Argyll. After five years working as a graphic artist, she now runs two self-catering holiday cottages which she and her partner converted from the farm steadings. The demands of family, garden and visitors conspire to keep her from writing but with her youngest son about to start school, she may be running out of excuses.

Carole Arnold lives in Surrey with her husband, two birth daughters, aged 22 and 18, a foster son, aged 14, a foster daughter, aged 15, and five cats. She has looked after and cared for, with assistance from the rest of the family, more than 40 young people, usually adolescents, in the past ten years. She job-shares as programme manager for a charity called Youth at Risk, currently working in Sutton, Surrey with young people involved in offending behaviour, drug or alcohol abuse, truanting or who have low self-esteem for a variety of reasons.

Anna Bell is a former nurse and currently lives in rural Somerset with her husband, who is a surgeon, and three sons. Since giving up her career to bring up the family, she has nevertheless retained a lively interest in medical matters and is currently pursuing an Open University degree whilst working part time as a counsellor. A strong urge to help her own sixteen–year–old son through a difficult psychological period recently drew her toward relating her experience in words.

Rosalind Brackenbury lives happily in Key West, Florida, with her American husband. She has recently published a fourth poetry collection, *The Beautiful Routes Of The West* (1996) and has finished a new novel. She writes regularly for *Resurgence* and teaches a class for unblocking artists in Key West. Her son, Sam Brackenbury, moved recently from London to Sunderland, Tyne & Wear, and has been writing his autobiography, *Runaway Boy*, and working with young offenders.

Kate Bromfield lives in South–East London with her husband and two teenaged children. She is an ex–teacher who now spends much of her spare time reading and writing short stories, some of which have been short–listed in competitions. Her autobiographical piece 'My Brilliant Career!' is published in *Mustn't Grumble: Writing by Disabled Women*, edited by Lois Keith (The Women's Press, 1994).

Jean Buffong was born on the island of Grenada in the Caribbean. England has been her home for the past 34 years. Now that her family has grown up, her time is split between being a full–time civil servant, an established writer and a community worker. Jean's novels, *Under the Silk Cotton Tree* (1992) and *Snowflakes in the Sun* (1995) are published by The Women's Press, as is her novella, *Jump-Up-and-Kiss-Me*, which appears together with Nellie Payne's *A Grenadian Childhood in Jump-Up-and-Kiss-Me: Two Stories from Grenada* (1990). Her work can also be found in *The Women's Press Book of New Myth and Magic* (1993), *Mango 'n' Spice* and *Heresay*.

Julia Buxton is in her early forties. She lives in the suburbs of a large city and works in the administration department of a college of higher education. She has two children – Lucy, about whom she has written, and Ben, an older son who seems to have his life sorted out (lucky boy) and has set up home with his girlfriend. Julia and her husband (from whom she is separated and who lives on his own) have a good relationship and there is even talk of a reconciliation.

Kate Cargreaves is a developing freelance writer living in the East Midlands. She has worked in the statutory and voluntary welfare sectors. Her first book, *Journey To Our Children*, is the personal account of infertility and the adoption of her children. For many years she has had chronic ME and is committed to the disability rights movement. She is inspired by Celtic spirituality and the works of Mother Julian of Norwich. She is married to a probation officer and has a son of thirteen and a daughter of nine.

Elizabeth Fraser lives in South West Scotland. She has two daughters now aged 16 and 20. The eldest has left home and is currently unemployed. The youngest lives at home and is studying art and design. Elizabeth is self-employed in the field of natural health therapies. She has published a small number of articles and poetry.

Diane Gibson is a 35-year-old mother of three adolescent sons. She has survived a marriage breakdown; after 16 years of torment and violence she moved to Edinburgh to start a new life. She has recently remarried and now feels she has all the love and support she needs to survive the next few years of her sons' adolescence.

Carolyn Giles lives in Northamptonshire where she is a self-employed training and development consultant, often (heavily!) involved in National Vocational Qualifications. She has a daughter who is now 21 and a son of 18. Carolyn is pleased to say that both are now flying free.

Meg Graham lives in Scotland and is the mother of five children. A survivor of an abusive marriage, she has gone on to help other abused women through her work as a counsellor for Women's Aid and remains deeply committed to women's issues.

Marie Guise Williams is a writer and broadcast journalist. She graduated in 1995 with a BA in Media and Communications. Until recently she was widely known as Marie Evans, and under her former name she performed her work throughout the North West, the Midlands and further afield. She also runs creative writing classes for women in the North West. Marie Guise Williams is published widely, including in *Dancing On Diamonds* (1993), an anthology of the best young writers in the North West, and is currently working on a collection of short stories, as well as her début novel.

Hazell Hills has spent most of her life in Birmingham, England – apart from 7 years in New Zealand in the 1960s. She has worked as a freelance writer, full-time English lecturer, college counsellor, mother and wife. She has published poems and short stories in a variety of magazines and anthologies in Britain and New Zealand. Hazell Hills has 4 'homemade' children, 2 inherited stepsons, and 5 grandchildren.

Helena Hinn has been widely anthologised in many women's journals and anthologies including the *Virago Book of Birth Poetry*, *The West in her Eye*, and *The Common Thread*. She had a poetry collection published in 1994, and has also written a novel and a book of short stories. She was born in 1958, trained at art college and is the mother of two children and the part-time stepmother of two more.

Isobel has been a mother and foster mother for nearly forty years. Now an ancient, battered grandmother, she remains reasonably sane, and can still remember the shock of her first experience of living with adolescent problems.

Pamela Lewis started writing as a freelance journalist in the early 1960s, before turning to writing poetry. As a wife and mother, and later returning to practice as a part-time occupational therapist, time was short for writing. Taking what was to hand as source material, she has written an autobiography of her family life in poetry over the last thirty years. The daughter of the poem is now an international bond dealer and the son a banker. Her younger daughter has recently started writing. Pamela's writing has been widely published and broadcast, and two collections of her work have appeared, *One Mile from the Centre* (1971) and *Admissions* (1987).

Caeia March was born in the Isle of Man in 1946 and grew up in industrial South Yorkshire. She came out as a lesbian in October 1980, and she has two grown-up sons aged 22 and 20. She lives in Cornwall. She is a countrywoman now and is a very keen gardener. She has published poetry, short stories and non-fiction articles and is widely known as a tutor of women's studies and creative writing. She is the author of five novels, all published by The Women's Press, *Three Ply Yarn* (1986), *The Hide and Seek Files* (1988), *Fire! Fire!* (1991), *Reflections* (1995) and *Between the Worlds* (1996).

Emma Marx lives and writes in the USA. She teaches writing to college students and publishes poetry and short fiction in literary magazines and journals. Emma Marx has been married for sixteen years and has two step-sons.

Diana Mason is 44 and lives in Somerset. She graduated in 1996 from the University of Wales, College of Cardiff, with a Creative Writing MA and a large overdraft. She won the 'One Voice Monologue Competition' in 1995, various poetry competition awards, and is published in *Blasters: Love Life*, a collection of short stories.

Liz Morgan has been involved with children for most of her life and found great pleasure in caring for them. She is a northerner and was married for many years. Since her husband's death her main hobby has been creative writing. She had an article published in *Woman* magazine in 1990, has been published in anthologies, and is now working on a novel.

Colette O'Hare, originally from Belfast, lives in West London. At one time a feature writer for women's magazines, she now writes and teaches part-time in adult education. She has had many short stories and two children's books published. She has four sons.

Barbie Ordish shares a household in North West London with her youngest daughter, three dogs, two chinchillas, a rat and a ferret. She works full-time as a receptionist, and her hobbies include running around Hampstead Heath with the dogs at ridiculous hours of the morning and moaning about not having enough time to write. In December 1995 a play she wrote about London Zoo was performed there, to great in-house acclaim. Her ambition is to become rich enough to get her car through its MOT and buy carpet for the stairs.

Elisavietta Ritchie's Flying Time: Stories & Half-Stories includes four PEN Syndicated Fiction winners. Among her poetry collections are: *The Arc of the Storm, Elegy for the Other Woman, Tightening The Circle Over Eel Country, Raking the Snow* and *Wild Garlic: The Journal of Maria X*. She edited *The Dolphin's Arc: Endangered Creatures of the Sea*. Her work appears in *Poetry*,

American Scholar, New York Times, Christian Science Monitor, Washington Post, several Papier-Mache anthologies and numerous other publications in the US and abroad.

Jill Robinson lives with her two sons, Tom and Alex, in Yorkshire. She trained as a teacher, but has for many years worked with various voluntary organisations such as Citizen's Advice Bureaux and the Alzheimer's Disease Society. She has contributed articles to several journals, both national and local, and for three years wrote an advice column for a local newspaper. She is currently studying for a Masters degree in Social Studies at Bradford, and doing voluntary work for the local Victim Support scheme.

Jiffy Sandison trained as a painter and etcher. She now teaches in a large, London comprehensive school where her focus is on ensuring bilingual pupils have access to the curriculum. Jiffy's current passion is writing short stories, and attending a writers' group regularly helps her keep up the discipline required.

Diana Scott lives in rural Scotland where her main focus is at present counselling, though writing, organising politically and spiritual spaces are also squeezed in somehow. Her daughter is now 21 and lives in Edinburgh, and her 15-year-old son is still at home.

Lynne Smith lives in West Yorkshire where she works as an adult education tutor. She enjoys freelance writing and looking after her numerous cats.

Ruth Smith is married, with three grown-up children and lives with her husband in Bromley, Kent. Her children also live in the London area. One manages drugs centres, another divides her time between conservation and computer graphics, and the third plays guitar in a band. Until last summer she taught

English in a secondary school for girls but a back injury brought about an early retirement. She has been writing poetry for twenty months now and has been published in several poetry magazines including *Poetry Digest*, *Rivet*, *First Time*, and in winners' anthologies, printed as an outcome of national poetry competitions. One of her poems travelled round London for six months as part of a 'Poetry on the Buses' venture organised jointly by Big, Wide Words and Friends Of The Earth.

Frances Viner is an artist who writes, acts and directs. Her first play, *Viva Peckham*, was premiered at the Etcetera Theatre Club in 1996, and she is currently working on a one-woman show, *Bitch's Dinner*. Frances is also a director of City Artworks which produces music theatre with young people. She is sustained by the love of her two children, Alexandra and Oscar, and that of many extraordinary friends.

Maggie Woods is a journalist working in London. Both her sons are at art college. She has 13 non-fiction books published and, now that her boys appear to have become independent, is about to set off in a new direction, living in the country and writing fiction.

Sara Yeomans was born in 1943 in Gloucestershire, and grew up there. In 1961 she was one of the first fifty-two students to go to Sussex University, where she studied English and gained a degree in 1964. She has also studied theatre direction and has worked as a teacher, a scriptwriter and director, a freelance writer and journalist, and as assistant editor on the magazine *Devon Life*. She is the author of *Travels with a Pram and Hot Flush and the Toy Boy* (The Women's Press, 1994). Sara Yeomans has three daughters and lives and works in Devon.